MW01286623

1

The Royal House of Stewart

David Peters

© 2014 David Peters

ISBN 9781503024120

Other titles by the same author

"On The Whole......" ISBN 9781484106334

(Paperback) & ASIN B00LMN84GG (KDP)

"Scotland's Military History" ISBN
9781490449227 & ASIN B00DQBT01U

"The Brotherhood" ISBN 9781492977742 & ASIN
B00H54HZGQ

"The Haunting" ISBN 9781500197551 & ASIN
B00LXGS4JO

"India from Mughal Empire to Independence"
ISBN 9781508995623 & ASIN B00WFI0Q7C

Contents Pages

A Foreword

This literary offering is about the Scottish family of Stewart. No other single family has had the same influence on the histories of Scotland, Great Britain and the United Kingdom as they have had, and not all of it was good! Up to the early 17th Century the separate monarchies of Scotland and England had been engaged in an almost continual battle for supremacy for hundreds of years, the balance of power swinging first one way and then the other, though to be honest, England probably just edged it over the piece!   James VI then, consciously or unconsciously, acknowledged this fact I think, when he inherited the English crown in 1603 and promptly decided to up root himself and his court, moving lock, stock and barrel from Edinburgh to London and what he obviously saw as the seat of power of the "senior" of the two Kingdoms.   Despite many promises to the contrary, he made only the one fleeting visit back to the land of his birth between then and his death in 1625; and his son, Charles I and grandsons, Charles II and James II, are all on record at various times since then as stating that they "had little or no time for Scotland or the Scots"! Thus the family, rather shamefully, forsook their Scots heritage from the time of the union of the crowns and became, on a personal level at least, very much English orientated from then on!

Although the title of this book, or historical chronicle, call it what you will, is "The Royal House of Stewart", I decided to initiate my account of this most fascinating and captivating, not to mention bloody, period of Scottish and British history a wee bit earlier, in 1292 to be exact, with the inauguration of King John Balliol which followed on from a two year interregnum. The events which occurred from then on more or less set the scene for what was to come over the next seventy five years in particular. This covers a second ten year interregnum between the reigns of John Balliol and Robert the Bruce as well as the sixty five year tenure of the Scottish throne by the House of Bruce beginning on the 25th of March 1306 with the crowning of Robert the Bruce, to the death of his son, and successor, King David II on the 22nd of February 1371.

On that date in February 1371, the throne was inherited by King Robert II who was the precursor of the long running Stewart dynasty and grandson of Robert the Bruce, courtesy of his mother, Bruce's daughter Marjorie. His father was Walter Stewart, the 6th High Steward of Scotland and who had fought at Bannockburn with The Bruce, commanding, with Douglas, the left flank of his victorious army. The House of Stewart then continued an almost unbroken reign, in Scotland anyway – apart from the nine years from 1651 to 1660 when Charles II was in exile - from then until the death of Queen Anne on the 1st of August 1714. This covered some 343 years, fifteen Monarchs and was not always a time of peace and tranquillity. They ruled in Scotland, England, Ireland and Great Britain progressively over the years and of the fourteen Stewart monarchs - Mary II's husband and co-ruler William of Orange was a Stewart only on his mother's side - one was murdered, one died violently by accident, one died in exile, one was executed, two died in battle, two abdicated and the other six died natural deaths! Incidentally, the crest on the front cover of the book is the crest of the Royal coat of arms of Scotland, depicting the Honours of Scotland: Crown, Sword and Sceptre! See the brief account dealing with these in chapter eleven.

Broadly speaking, the Stewart monarchs, and the Bruce's as well for that matter, were maybe just a shade less than the honest and upright human beings they purported to be; they were probably the perpetrators, and the victims, of more subterfuge and skulduggery than all of the plots of the 21st century TV soap operas combined! Some of the males of the dynasty, Robert II and Charles II immediately come to mind here, were also responsible for sowing more wild oats - as well as not a few legitimate ones, at least in Robert's case - than the accumulative efforts of the US mid-western farmers today! They were basically an egotistical bunch, including the ladies, wrapped up in their own self-importance and generally convinced that they knew better than anyone else. This made them unwilling to council, or be counselled by any other, possibly better informed individuals than themselves, and were therefore, a pretty partisan bunch in their opinions, a behavioural condition which often cost them dear down the ages! Charles I, I think, particularly epitomises this egotistical attitude as it cost him his life!

With the demise of Queen Anne, the throne passed to the House of Hanover and George I, a great-grandson of James VI & I, pursuant to the "Act of Settlement 1701" which decreed that the

British Crown had to be inherited by a Protestant, regardless of any stronger Catholic claims! (I Wonder what the P.C. brigade would make of all that today)? And there were many such claims, including Anne's half-brother, James Francis Edward Stuart, better known as "The Old Pretender" and father of Bonnie Prince Charlie. Note the change of spelling here from "Stewart" to "Stuart". This was brought about by Mary I, Queen of Scots 1542 – 1567, who was executed in 1587 and who spent her childhood at the French Court; she was wed to the Dauphin, Francis in 1558 two years before his death in 1560 and upon which Mary returned to Scotland. This is probably when the name change took place and for no other reason than the letter "W" does not exist in the French alphabet! Broadly speaking, "Stewart" is the accepted form of address for the dynasty before the Union of the Crowns in 1603 and "Stuart" for afterwards, although there is nothing to say that it can't be left up to one's personal preference. Personally, I chose to stick with "Stewart" throughout this chronicle as I tend to be a traditionalist by nature! (See "footnote").

Another point I'd like to clarify at this stage is the fact that throughout this book the reader may well come across what, at first sight; appear to be confusing references to some of the titled Lords of the land and at various times in the narration. This is not due to a particular titular Lord enjoying a prolonged life of a hundred years or more, it is down to the fact that several of the hereditary titles of Scotland went through many creations of that title, in particular the Dukedom of Albany with seven or eight creations over a four hundred year span; and the Earldom of Moray with five creations covering some two hundred and fifty years. Therefore, when I refer to the "1st Earl of Moray" for instance, in two different places and many years apart, I'm referring to two different men and not a single nonagenarian enjoying a Methuselahistic lifespan!

There are also a lot of "heavy politics" involved throughout the Stewart reign particularly after the Union of the Crowns, namely the Bill of Rights of 1689 and its Scottish equivalent the Claim of Rights of the same year, the Act of Settlement of 1701, the Act of Security (Scotland) of 1704 and the Acts of Union of 1706 & 1707; these will be dealt with in chronological order as we arrive at these particular periods. Also included, although strictly speaking out - with the scope of this book, is the Acts of Union of 1800, which is really just an exercise in crossing the T's and dotting the I's in the history of these British Isles. I have tried to keep all the information which makes up this book brief, in an attempt to keep it interesting, while retaining accuracy, which is, of course, a prerequisite, again, see "footnote". I have also made a serious attempt to remain objective, non-judgemental and unopinionated which are very difficult combinations to achieve and I can only hope the reader considers me to have been successful, anyway, into the breach, as they say - - - -

King John Balliol 1292 – 1296

John was crowned as King of Scotland, on Edward of England's recommendation, at Scone on the 30th of November 1292 thus ending the two year long first period of Interregnum in Scotland between the demise of Margaret, Maid of Norway and himself. He reigned until his enforced abdication at Stracathro, near Montrose, on the 10th of July 1296, thus beginning the ten year long second period of Interregnum between himself and Robert the Bruce. An "Interregnum" being the official term for a period of time between the end of one monarch's reign and the start of the next! Taking Balliol's dismal track record into account, we could almost stretch a point here and claim that in fact, there was only the one Interregnum, starting in 1290 and lasting to 1306 but that would be historically inaccurate at best, and a wee bit unfair on John B, not to say maybe a wee bit cruel as well! I say this because in my opinion, the Scottish parliament of the day was guilty of a huge error of judgement in inviting an over-aggressive megalomaniac to interfere in their affairs of state! King John, not the strongest or most determined of men, was also extremely unlucky to be pitted against one of, if not the, strongest English Kings ever. During Balliol's reign and the second Interregnum Scotland was virtually ruled remotely by this man, Edward I of England!

Not a lot is known about King John's early life, he was born between 1248 and 1250 and it is not even certain if this event occurred in Scotland, England or France, such is the lack of information. He was the son of John, 5th Baron Balliol, Lord of Barnard Castle and his wife Dervorguilla of Galloway, daughter of the Lord of Galloway and granddaughter of the Earl of Huntingdon. He inherited significant lands in Galloway, various English and Scottish estates of the Huntingdon Earldom from his mother, and large estates in England and France from his father, so he was already a very wealthy man, independently of his Royal status.

It all began in 1284 when a parliament at Scone recognized Margaret, Maid of Norway, who was the daughter of Eric II, King of Norway and Margaret, daughter of King Alexander III of Scotland, as heiress to the Scottish throne. Alexander's death in 1286 was without issue and left the throne in the possession of the then three year old Margaret, born on the 9th of April 1283, and whose mother had died giving birth to her. It also left the country under the rule of the guardians of Scotland for the duration of her minority. Following Margaret's premature death in 1290 in Orkney, en-route to Scotland, and which left the country without an undisputed successor, Balliol became a competitor for the vacant crown in what became known as the "Great Cause" along with Robert Bruce, 5th Lord of Annandale and grandfather of Robert the Bruce, who was later destined to claim the monarchy for his own. Two other claimants for the vacant crown during the great cause have disappeared into the mists of time; they were Floris V, Count of Holland and John De Hastings of Abergavenny, 2nd Baron Hastings, as being the only other men who could prove descent from King David I.

To go back a century and a half, David I, 1124 – 1153 was the fourth son of Malcolm Canmore (King Malcolm III 1058 -1093), and was the monarch who came up with the unique idea of "importing" men he could trust from England to keep the King's peace in Scotland and in return for which they received lands and homes. He was able to do this as he was on good terms with the then English King Henry I, 1100 – 1135, who was the fourth son of William the Conqueror! These men were mostly knights of noble Norman birth who had come over with William in 1066 with names like *De Brus*, which Anglicised into the famous Bruce! David's father, Malcolm, was the monarch who, no doubt under duress and having been comprehensively defeated in battle by William the Conqueror - who had by now totally subjugated England and made himself King in the process - signed the Treaty of Abernethy in 1072, acknowledging William as his feudal overlord and thus created a very dangerous and a very troublesome precedent for all the Scottish monarchs who were to come after him! Edward I was to make full use of this historical point of fact two hundred and twenty years later in his political manipulations with the Scottish Crown!

To continue, prior to the Maid of Norway's death, the guardians of Scotland had drawn up the "Treaty of Birgham" in 1290 and which was basically a marriage contract between her and the five year old Edward of Caernarvon, heir to the English throne and the future Edward II. A secondary purpose of the treaty was to put to rest the competing claims of the Houses of Balliol and Bruce which were nearing open hostility. The treaty also contained the interesting proviso that even though the Royal Houses of England and Scotland were to be joined in marriage, Scotland should remain "separate, apart and free from any subjugation from England"! It also stated that the Churches and Parliaments of the two countries should remain independent of each other. Clearly the intent here was to keep Scotland as an independent entity in everything bar her monarchy. The treaty however was to prove hypothetical with the premature death of the Maid of Norway in 1290 and Edward I didn't lose any time in capitalising on this. In 1291 he "requested" that the Scottish nobles meet him at Norham on Tweed whereupon he styled himself "Lord Paramount of Scotland" and challenged the claimants to the throne to recognise him as their feudal superior! He achieved this by virtue of the facts that he had his army ready to hand, the Scots had no King, no army ready and only three weeks to accept Edward's terms or else!

All this resulted in Balliol allying himself with the Bishop of Durham who was the representative of Edward I in Scotland, and styling himself the "heir of Scotland". Bruce meanwhile, had arrived at the site where Margaret's proposed inauguration was to have been, at the head of a considerable military force and amidst rumours that his friends, the Earls of Mar and Atholl were also rallying their forces. The country was headed for civil war! To avoid this, in early 1292 Edward was asked to intervene as arbitrator. Edward - second ruler of the House of Plantagenet and known as "Longshanks" because of his long legs, and later on as the "Hammer of the Scots" - along with the Scottish auditors duly announced their decision on the 17th of November 1292 in the Great Hall of Berwick Castle. John Balliol was named King of Scotland and was crowned thus two weeks later.

All this while however, and behind the scenes, Edward was relentlessly pursuing his hidden agenda of creating a British Empire dominated by England, and to this end had deliberately aligned himself behind Balliol who, in his view, was the weaker and more malleable of the two contenders for the Scottish throne. He had also previously coerced recognition for himself as Lord Paramount of Scotland, feudal superior of the realm, as per the terms of the Treaty of Abernethy, and then as such, steadily proceeded to undermine Balliol's authority at every turn! Amongst other things, he demanded homage to be paid towards himself, contributions towards the costs for the defence of England and military support from the Scots for his ongoing war with France. In short, he treated Scotland as a feudal vassal state and repeatedly humiliated its new King.

Incidentally, the first known official Scottish parliamentary rolls ever, dates from the first parliament of John Balliol in February 1293 and is a record of what happened there. Balliol's seal was attached to the documents as a sign of Royal approval! The first known mention of a Scottish parliament at all, dates from 1235 and refers to an assembly held at Kirkliston, a small burgh just outside Edinburgh, and was an evolution of the "King's great council" which were gatherings of Churchmen and nobles who advised the King on policy and justice measures. The first known burgh's and the introduction of coinage occurred in Scotland just prior to this, around the mid twelfth century.

The Scots however, very soon tired of their deeply compromised King and the leading men of the Kingdom moved to take affairs out of Balliol's hands by appointing a new panel of guardians at Stirling in July 1295. This panel went on to conclude a treaty of mutual assistance with France, to be known later as the "Auld Alliance". A highly displeased Edward retaliated to all this by initiating the Wars of Scottish Independence and invading Scotland. First of all he committed heinous crimes against humanity by sacking Berwick upon Tweed with the wholesale slaughter of the largely innocent populace, and then taking Dunbar Castle on the 27th of April 1296. King John was forced to abdicate at Stracathro, near Montrose on the 10th of July 1296; here the Arms of Scotland were formally torn from his surcoat giving rise to the everlasting slur of "Toom Tabbard" or "empty coat or jacket"!

The deposed and disgraced monarch was imprisoned in the Tower of London until he was allowed to go to France in 1299. When his baggage was examined at Dover however, by what can only be termed as an extremely efficient predecessor of our modern day customs & excise officers, it was found to contain the Royal Golden Crown and Seal of the Kingdom of Scotland, much gold and silver and a not inconsiderable sum of money as well. John obviously considered himself worthy of a redundancy payment that only today's bankers can dream of or compare to, and in return for a similar level of commitment to boot! Edward bequeathed the crown to St. Thomas the Martyr, kept the seal for himself, allowed John to keep the money and who knows what happened to the gold and silver? John was released into the custody of Pope Boniface VIII on the condition that he remained at a Papal residence; he was in turn released from this jurisdiction around the summer of 1301 where he saw out the rest of his days, in ignominy, on his family's ancestral estates at Helicourt in Picardy, which lies north east of Paris, France.

After 1302 he made no further attempt to extend his personal support to the Scots; this effectively meant that Scotland was without a monarch until the accession of Robert the Bruce in 1306! John died on the 25th of November 1314, exactly five months after Bruce's momentous victory at Bannockburn. He left a son, Edward Balliol, who was to cause all sorts of trouble for the Scots in general and Bruce's son, King David II in particular, between 1332 and 1337. Backed by his friend, Edward III of England, Balliol led incursions into Scotland, made himself a pretender for the Scottish throne and indeed, at one point became King, albeit on a "de facto" basis. He was finally hounded out for good by David's guardian, Sir Andrew Murray in 1337! The actions of Balliol and Edward III instigated the start of the second Scottish War of Independence in 1332, a mere four years after the end of the first, and this one was to last till 1357, well into the reign of Bruce's son, King David II.

Before all that however, between 1296 and 1306 there were several uprisings against Edward, who was in effect remotely ruling Scotland during that ten year interregnum between the reigns of Balliol and Bruce. The most significant of these was the one in 1297 led by William Wallace and Andrew Moray esquire, who had joined forces and gave the Hammer of the Scots a hammering at the Battle of Stirling Bridge on the 11th of September that year. A much smaller force of fewer than two and a half thousand bodies made intelligent use of the terrain to humiliate and put to flight, with heavy casualties, an army of some twelve thousand men. There is no record of the Scots casualties here but it's reckoned the English lost half their army on the field of battle that day.

Unfortunately, Moray died shortly afterwards of wounds sustained here while Wallace went on to become Sir William, and was appointed to the guardianship of Scotland for his efforts. He served as such until July 1298 when Edward exacted his revenge at the Battle of Falkirk and gave Wallace a hiding! In 1299 Wallace surrendered his guardianship to a joint one of Bruce and John Comyn who were protagonists at best and sworn enemies at worst! The Bishop of St Andrews, William De Lamberton, was elected as a third guardian in an attempt to try and keep the peace between the two of them! In August 1305 Wallace, who had more or less been in hiding since Falkirk but at one stage was reported to be in France fighting for the French against the English invaders, was captured near Glasgow and handed over to the English where he was charged with high treason and crimes against English civilians. This was surely a blatant exercise in dual standards and hypocrisy when one considers what Edward himself had been guilty of at Berwick upon Tweed nine years earlier, but for which Wallace was found guilty regardless and subsequently hung, drawn and quartered!   One man's freedom fighter is another man's terrorist!

The Bruce,

King Robert I, 1306 – 1329

Unquestionably the most famous, and probably the most enigmatic Scottish monarch of them all; how can we go about justifying an introduction like that? Well, let's have a go! For a start he was literally the grandfather of the prolific Stewart Dynasty, his daughter Marjorie, by his first wife Isabella of Mar, married Walter Stewart, 6th High Steward of Scotland, and their offspring became King Robert II, the precursor of a long line of Stewart monarchs and who inherited the throne in 1371 from his uncle, David II., Bruce's son by his second wife Elizabeth De Burgh, but more about them anon.

Bruce was descended from Scottish, Norman and Gaelic noble ancestry, being a 4X great grandson of King David I and also claimed Richard de Clare – 2nd Earl of Pembroke – King of Leinster and Governor of Ireland as well as Henry I of England among his paternal ancestors. His grandfather, also Robert de Brus, was the 5th Lord of

Annandale and one of the claimants to the Scottish throne, along with the eventual incumbent John Balliol, during the "Great Cause" of 1290 - 91. Bruce's father was the 6th Lord of Annandale and with his death in 1304, Bruce inherited his family's claim to the throne. He is fondly remembered today, along with Sir William Wallace, with something akin to hero worship, as a national hero as well as a great monarch.

Known in medieval Gaelic as "Roibert a Briuis", modern Gaelic as "Raibeart Bruis", Norman as "Robert de Brus" and early Scots as "Robert Brus"; Robert the Bruce, who was born on the 11th of July 1274 at Turnberry Castle, Ayrshire, was crowned as King of Scotland at Scone on the 25th of March 1306, thus bringing to an end Scotland's ten year long second period of Interregnum. He remained monarch until his death on the 7th of June 1329 at the Manor of Cardross, near Dumbarton. He was one of the most famous warriors of his generation - Wallace was obviously another - and eventually led Scotland against England during the first War of Scottish Independence. Initially though, both he and his grandfather supported Edward's invasion at the start of that war in 1296 in an attempt to force Balliol's abdication in revenge for that gentleman having had the temerity during his brief reign, to present the Bruce lands of Annandale to their deadly enemies, the Comyns and to whom Balliol was related through marriage!

One of the first blows to be struck in the Wars of Independence was a direct assault on the Bruce's. On the 26th of March 1296, several Scottish Earls, under the leadership of the Red Comyn, Lord of Badenoch and Lochaber, ably assisted by his father, the Black Comyn, his cousin John, the Earl of Buchan and sundry other relatives, attacked the Bruce stronghold of Carlisle, which had become their primary residence after the loss of their Annandale seat to the Comyn family, compliments of John Balliol. The Comyns already owned lands in Dalswinton and Nithsdale in the south west. The city was successfully defended by Bruce as the Comyns did not possess any siege engines or heavy artillery. Edward's response to the attack on Carlisle and King John's subsequent alliance with France was to launch a particularly brutal and bloody attack on Berwick upon Tweed at the end of March 1296 and where as many as 10,000 men women and children were indiscriminately and brutally slaughtered! This abomination was followed up by the Battle of Dunbar which effectively crushed all Scottish resistance and Balliol was subsequently deposed.

The said abdication achieved, Bruce swiftly changed sides again and indirectly threw his hand in with Wallace and Moray in their 1297 revolt by staging a similar event and raising his standard at Irvine. This failed, but explained the Bruce's absence at Wallace's great victory at Stirling Bridge and after which the future King chose to keep a low profile to gauge the repercussions of that battle. There is much dubiety about the Bruce's whereabouts, and part in, if any, at the Battle of Falkirk in 1298 where Wallace's army was crushed in retaliation for Stirling, and Wallace himself went underground until his capture in 1305. There are unconfirmed reports that Bruce actually fought for Edward against Wallace here but other, also unconfirmed reports have him at Ayr, sacking the town to deny its availability to the victorious English as they returned south.

Also in 1298 the future King became a guardian of Scotland but it was alongside his deadly enemy and rival for the throne, John Comyn. The Bishop of St. Andrews, William De Lamberton was elected as a third guardian, primarily to try and keep the peace between the other two as an arbiter. Bruce resigned the guardianship in 1300 jointly because of his quarrels with Comyn but also because it seemed for a while that Balliol might return. In 1302 however, he submitted to Edward and "returned to the King's peace" and in 1304, with his father's death, he inherited his family's claim to the throne. In 1303 Edward once again took his army north reaching first Edinburgh and then Perth, he then proceeded to Aberdeen via Dundee, Brechin and Montrose. Turning south again he headed for Dunfermline via Moray and Badenoch, thus effectively bringing the whole country under his submission. All the leading Scots except for William Wallace had surrendered to Edward by February 1304 and John Comyn, who was by now the sole guardian, also then submitted. With Scotland now defenceless, Edward set about destroying her as a realm. Homage was once again obtained by force from the nobles and the Aristocracy; and Scotland was once again subjugated by the English!

The Murder of John (the Red) Comyn

Like all of his family, Bruce had an unshakeable belief in his right to the throne, which appears to be a genetic trait he passed on to the Stewarts as it also seems to be inherent in them! However, by his continuous changes of political allegiance between the Scottish and English forces over the years, he had unintentionally nurtured a lot of mistrust towards his family. Some said he had changed sides more often than his apparel! Comyn on the other hand, had been much more resolute in his opposition to the English and as such, was singularly the most powerful noble in Scotland. Among his many powerful relations were the Earls of Buchan, Mar, Ross, Fife, Angus, Dunbar and Strathearn; the Lords of Kilbride, Kirkintulloch, Lenzie, Bedrule and Scraesburgh; plus the Sheriffs of Banff, Dingwall, Wigtown and Aberdeen. Not a man to be trifled with! He also had a strong claim to the throne through his descent from Donald III on his paternal side and David I on his maternal side. The Red Comyn was also the nephew of King John Balliol!

According to the records of the time which are at best questionable, and at worst pretty inaccurate, in late 1305 Comyn and Bruce entered into a signed, sealed and sworn agreement by which Comyn would agree to forfeit any claim to the throne in favour of Bruce - upon receipt of the Bruce lands in Scotland - should a successful uprising occur led by Bruce! Whether these details are correct or not, Edward, it is said, moved to arrest Bruce for this suspected plot while he was still a guest at the English Court. Luckily for Bruce, his friend Ralph de Mornthermer learnt of this and warned Bruce of Edward's intention by sending him 12 pennies and a pair of spurs! Bruce took this not-so-subtle hint and promptly fled the Court that night en-route for Scotland and that fateful meeting with John Comyn at the Abbey of Greyfriars in Dumfries.

Again according to records, Comyn had supposedly betrayed his agreement with Bruce to Edward, and when Bruce arranged a meeting for the 10th of February 1306 with Comyn at the Abbey in Dumfries and accused him of this treachery, they not surprisingly, came to blows. There are two versions of what happened next, the first and most popular one is that Bruce killed Comyn outright before the High Altar. The second one is that on being told Comyn had survived and was being treated for his injuries, two of Bruce's supporters, Roger de Kirkpatrick and John Lindsey, re-entered the Monastery and finished off Bruce's work. Regardless of which version is true, as far as Bruce was concerned, the "die was cast" and from that moment on and he had no option but to either become the King or to become a lifelong fugitive!

After making confession of his sacrilege and violence before Bishop Robert Wishart of Glasgow, Bruce was absolved of his crime but was still excommunicated by the Pope - at Edward's urging - for this deed. Bruce then moved quickly to seize the throne and was crowned King of Scots six weeks later on the 25th of March 1306 at Scone by Bishop William de

Lamberton of St Andrews and with all the formality and solemnity that such an occasion demanded. The Royal robes and Clerical Vestments which had been hidden from the English by Bishop Wishart were brought out and set upon the King. The great Lion Rampant of the King of Scotland, in use since 1222, was planted behind his throne and the Earls of Atholl, Mar, Lennox and Mentieth, amongst many others, made their allegiances to the newly crowned King, who, ironically, had had the crown placed upon his head by Isabella McDuff, Countess of Buchan and wife of John Comyn, 3rd Earl of Buchan who was a cousin to the murdered Red John Comyn!

In the June of 1306 Robert Bruce, 7th Earl of Carrick, Lord of Annandale and King of Scots was defeated in battle at Methven and two months later was surprised at Strathfillan where he had taken refuge. His wife and daughters and other women of the party were then sent to Kildrummy under the protection of his brother Neil and the Earl of Atholl. Bruce then, with a small company of his most faithful followers, including Sir James Douglas and Gilbert Hay, his brothers Thomas, Alexander and Edward, plus Sir Neil Campbell and the Earl of Lennox, fled. It is uncertain where Bruce and his small entourage spent the winter of 1306-07 but the Hebrides, Ireland, Orkney and Norway are all possibilities. The highly questionable, mythological legend of the spider in the cave probably stems from this period!

Meanwhile, Edward was marching north again in the spring of 1307. En-route he granted the Scottish estates of Bruce and his loyal followers to his own people and published a bill which excommunicated the King. Bruce's Queen Elizabeth, his daughter Marjorie, his sisters Christina and Mary, and Isabella McDuff were all captured in a sanctuary at Tain and sentenced to a harsh imprisonment. Mary and Isabella were suspended in cages at Roxburgh and Berwick Castles respectively for four years (one can only assume that this was done on a day-by-day basis) and Bruce's brother Neil was executed. On the 7th of July that year of 1307, Edward I, Hammer of the Scots, died of dysentery after a long deterioration leaving Bruce opposed by his son Edward II whom Bruce was destined to hand a most humiliating defeat to at Bannockburn some seven years later! As Balliol had been unlucky, Bruce was probably fortunate in that he was now up against a very much weaker man in Edward II, than his father Edward I had been!

Bruce and his followers returned to the Scottish Mainland in the spring of 1307 in two groups. The first, led by Bruce himself and his brother Edward landed at Turnberry Castle and began a William Wallace style guerrilla war in the south-west of the country. The second group, led by his brothers Thomas and Alexander, landed further south at Loch Ryan but were quickly captured and his brothers executed. In April, Bruce won the Battle of Glen Trool and followed that up with another victory at the Battle of Loudon Hill. Leaving his brother in command in Galloway, Bruce travelled north, capturing Inverlochy and Urquhart Castles, sacking Inverness Castle and Nairn and unsuccessfully threatening Elgin. He spent the rest of that year and all of the next, 1308, systematically overseeing the undoing of the Comyns by destroying their every stronghold, and therefore the power base, of that clan in northern and south-western Scotland. He was now close to ruling supreme!

In the March of 1309 he held his first parliament at St. Andrews and by August controlled all of Scotland north of the Tay. He was officially recognized as King and given the support of the Clergy of Scotland at the parliamentary session in March that year, and this support, given him by the Church in spite of his excommunication, was of immense political value! The next three years saw the capture and reduction of one English held stronghold after another, Douglas capturing Roxburgh and Randolph capturing Edinburgh. By the spring of 1314, Stirling Castle was the only strategic English stronghold left in Scotland and that was under siege by Edward Bruce! The Governor there, one Philip de Mowbray, agreed to surrender it to the Scots if he was not relieved by the 24th of June 1314.

These eight years of exhausting but deliberate refusal to meet the foe on even ground and level terms have caused many to consider Bruce to be one of the greatest guerrilla leaders of any age, including the Wallace! This must have represented a massive cultural change for one raised as a Feudal Knight, imbibed with all the rules of Chivalry! Unfortunately, this period of living rough was also to prove detrimental to his health in later years.

The Battle of Bannockburn

Around Lent of thirteen fourteen, Stirling Castle was still under the command of Sir Philip Mowbray and also under siege by Edward Bruce, the King's brother. Little headway was being made in this undertaking however and agreement was reached by the protagonists' that if no relief arrived from England by midsummer, then the Castle would be surrendered to Bruce. King Edward II left Berwick upon Tweed on the seventeenth of June at the head of an impressive army of some eighteen thousand foot and five thousand cavalry, approximately fifteen hundred of whom were of the heavy variety and Knights of the realm! Edward's preliminary objective was the relief of Stirling Castle of course, but the real reason for his incursion into Scotland was to try to put an end to the guerrilla warfare waged by Bruce and defeat him and his Scottish army in the field, face-to-face and thereby end the ongoing hostilities between the two Countries.

Bruce's army was eight thousand strong, mainly infantry armed with long spears and a small force of light cavalry. As well as the English King, Bruce was also up against some of his most irreconcilable enemies in Edward's ranks, the Earl of Angus Ingram De Umfraville, a former guardian of Scotland and his kinsmen as well as some others of various clans. Also into this category came Sir John Comyn of Badenoch, son of the Red Comyn whom Bruce had killed at Greyfriars Kirk in Dumfries in thirteen hundred and six. While it was not unusual for the Bruce's and the Comyns to find themselves at each other's throats, it was unusual to find the Comyns and the English on the same side. Sir John, along with a great many of the English hierarchy, did not survive the two day battle which in itself was an anomaly, as the majority of armed confrontations in these days very rarely lasted more than a day, if that.

Bruce's intelligent deployment of his forces, outnumbered three to one, and his use of the prevalent marshy and watery terrain in the area, went a long way to nullifying Edward's heavy cavalry in particular as well as his heavy infantry. The highlight of that first day of battle, before a shot was fired so to speak, and to many a precursor of what was to follow, was the meeting of Bruce and Sir Henry De Bohun in single combat. De Bohun, spotting Bruce was on his own from some distance away, lowered his lance point and charged. Bruce waited till he was only feet away then raised himself in his stirrups and swung his battleaxe at De Bohun's head splitting his helmet, and his skull, asunder! This led, as one could imagine, to the Scots taking the honours on that first day with more than a few victorious assaults on the English positions.

At the start of the second day of hostilities, Edward made his worst decision of all, he ordered his army to start crossing the Bannockburn! Seeing this, the Scots spearmen started to advance, repulsing an attack by English cavalry led by the Earl of Gloucester who perished along with most of his men trying to prevent this. The very size and strength of Edward's army was now beginning to work against him, it was unwieldy and cumbersome, slow to manoeuvre and unable to take up any positions, defensive or otherwise, and lacked proper leadership. Seeing this, Bruce committed his entire agile and fast moving force in a full frontal attack on the heaving, immobile mass of English soldiery causing great slaughter.

The English broke and ran and a great roar went up from the Scots; on hearing this, the Scots camp followers grabbed what weapons they could and ran to join the main army. When the English saw this they thought it was a second assault by a fresh force and total panic set in. Hundreds drowned as they re-crossed the Bannockburn and thousands more died crushed and trampled underfoot by their own men and all the while the Scots were attacking and slaughtering the hindmost of the English. Edward had by now fled the field with his personal bodyguard and the whole thing turned into a complete and utter rout!

The English suffered sixty five per cent casualties, some twelve or thirteen thousand men in all, including all their heavy cavalry and most of the light against a mere two thousand fallen Scots. As was to happen one hundred and ninety nine years later at Flodden, but in reverse, the much stronger and better equipped force was put to the sword and humiliated by a much smaller but better led and organized force determined to give a good account of themselves whatever the outcome at the end of the day. Though where the English humiliation here at Bannockburn took two days, the similar humiliation of the Scots at Flodden almost two centuries later only took about three hours!

However, back to 1314; the overwhelming victory here by the Scots confirmed the re-establishment of an independent Scottish monarchy. Scotland's armies were now free to launch devastating raids into northern England virtually at will. Deciding to expand the war against the English, Bruce now decided to open a second front in 1315 by sending his brother Edward, with a small army, to Ireland to appeal to the Irish to rise against Edward II's rule there. The Irish crowned Edward Bruce as High King of Ireland in 1316 and King Robert the Bruce later went there with another army to assist his brother as a strong contingent of supporters of Balliol and Comyn had ensconced themselves there under John McDougall of Lorn after Bannockburn and were, therefore, still a threat to Bruce.

The Bruce campaign in Ireland was characterised by some initial success but the Scots failed to win over the non-Ulster chiefs from the south who, quite rightly, couldn't see the difference between Scottish or English occupation. The Scots were eventually defeated by the English, and Bruce's last surviving brother, Edward, perished at the Battle of Faughart or Dundalk on the 14th of October 1318. This result went down in the history of the period as one the best things to happen for the Irish nation as it brought to an end the famine and pillaging of the Irish by both the Scots and the English!

Despite Bannockburn and the capture of the final English stronghold at Berwick in 1318, Edward II still refused to give up his claim to overlordship of Scotland, causing the Scottish magnates and nobles to submit the Declaration of Arbroath to Pope John XXII in 1320 declaring the Bruce as their rightful King and asserting Scotland's status as an independent Kingdom. The Pope finally recognized Scotland's independence in 1328 and simultaneously lifted Bruce's excommunication. Previously, in 1326 the Franco-Scottish alliance had been renewed in the treaty of Corbeil and in 1327 the English deposed Edward II in favour of his son Edward III who duly signed the Edinburgh-Northampton treaty, by which he renounced all claims to superiority over Scotland as well as agreeing to return the Stone of Destiny, which was later reneged upon! Thus ended the first War of Scottish Independence!

Prior to his death Bruce had been suffering from a serious illness from at least 1327, which more than one source claimed to be leprosy. In these days however, virtually any skin disease was erroneously attributed to this malady. Whatever it was, it was more than likely attributable to the long-term effects of his years of wandering and living rough between 1306 and 1309, this points to tuberculosis or other respiratory and lung related diseases in particular, although syphilis can't be ruled out either. Other possibilities are motor neurone disease or a series of strokes. Whatever it was, there is no record of him being quarantined from his fellow man at any time or for any reason.

Bruce's last journey, in early 1329, appears to have been a pilgrimage to the Shrine of St. Ninian at Whithorn and was probably in search of a miraculous cure or to make peace with God, or a combination of both. He also stayed at, or visited, Glenluce Abbey and Monreith from whence he visited St Ninian's cave. He stayed at the Shrine, fasting for four or five days and praying, before returning by sea to his Manor of Cardross, near Dumbarton. His final wish here at Cardross before he died was that his heart be cut from his body and borne on a crusade to the Holy Land before being returned to Scotland!

King Robert I died on the 7th of June 1329. His body was buried in Dunfermline Abbey while his heart was eventually interred in Melrose Abbey.

Sir James Douglas had agreed to take the King's embalmed heart on a crusade to the Lord's Sepulchre in the Holy Land but only managed to reach as far as Grenada where he died in battle. Sir William Keith of Galston and Sir Symon Lockhart of Lee conveyed the Heart back to Scotland.

Bruce died utterly fulfilled with his families unchallenged right to the throne firmly established and the Kingdom safe in the hands of his most trusted lieutenant, Sir Thomas Randolph the 1st Earl of Moray – first creation - who had been appointed guardian of Scotland by the Act of Settlement 1318. The intention was for him to remain so until Bruce's infant son David reached adulthood. His life's work was consolidated by the issue of Papal Bulls from Rome (letters or charters of importance) granting the privilege of Unction (sacramental anointment) at the coronations of all the future monarchs of Scotland!

The Discovery of the Bruce's Tomb

On the 17th of February 1818 men working on the new parish Church to be built on the site of the eastern choir of Dunfermline Abbey discovered a vault lying in front of the former Abbey's high altar. This was covered by two big flat slabs, one as a headstone and the other six feet in length with six iron rings set in it. The vault below was seven feet long, two feet wide and eighteen inches deep. Within lay the remnants of a rotted oak coffin with a body entirely encased in lead inside it! The site was closed up and guarded until the 5th of November 1819 when further investigation took place.

The body was then raised up and placed on a wooden board, the lead was removed and the remains inspected by experts. Its sternum had been sawn open from top to bottom to facilitate the removal of the heart after death; this removed any lingering doubt as to its identity! Further investigation revealed that the Bruce would have stood six feet and one inch in height in his youth, which, by medieval standards was impressive. The remains were then placed in a new lead coffin into which was poured several hundredweights of molten tar as a preservative and then sealed. The whole was then ceremoniously re-interred in the vault from whence it came to become the last resting place of probably Scotland's most famous son and the founding father of a dynasty which was to prevail until the 1st day of August 1714, or almost three and a half centuries!

David Bruce, King David II, 1329-1371

David, the Bruce's son, had a virtually impossible act to follow. No matter what he did, attempted to do, or could even actually achieve for that matter, he would never measure up to his father, far less fill his boots! He was on a hiding to nothing before a ball was kicked, to put the situation into a modern day footballing parlance! We can only surmise for whatever reason, that the Bruce chose to name his son, by his second wife Elizabeth de Burgh, after his 4G grandfather King David I of Scotland, of the House of Canmore and who had reigned from 1124 until his death on the 24th of May 1153. The hapless David was forced to deal with three major issues during his reign; the first was his own nobles, some of whom had been appointed as guardians during his minority and included the powerful Douglas's. The second threat was Edward Balliol, son of "Toom Tabbard" and the third was the English King, Edward III, patron and ally of Balliol.

The future King was born on the 5th of March 1324 at Dunfermline Palace in Fife which is today, and has been for almost 400 years, a ruin and now under the care of "Historic Scotland". He was married at Berwick-upon-Tweed on the 17th of July 1328, aged four, to Joan of the tower, a more mature aged seven, who was the daughter of Edward II and born on the 5th of July1321. This union was as laid down in the terms of the Edinburgh – Northampton treaty which was written in French, signed in Edinburgh by Robert the Bruce, ratified in Northampton by the English parliament and brought to an end the first War of Scottish Independence on the 17th of March 1328! David inherited his father's crown upon his death on the 7th of June 1329 and his Coronation was on the 24th of November 1331 at Scone where he was the first Scottish King to be anointed as per the Papal Bulls of the 13th of July 1329 granting Unction. He died unexpectedly at Edinburgh Castle on the 22nd of February 1371 aged 46 and without issue. David was also a different kettle of fish from his father; he was more content to let life happen to him as opposed to the Bruce who had tended to grab it by the throat!

The English didn't waste any time in stirring up bad feeling again by trying to take advantage of

David's minority with several attempts to replace him with Edward Balliol, son of "Toom Tabbard", who was a protégé of Edward III and a pretender to the Scottish throne. It should be remembered that David II, the younger of the two by twelve years, and Edward were brother's-in-law by David's marriage to Edward's sister Joan as children. Not only did Edward decide to support Balliol's claim over David's, he also chose to keep the Stone of Destiny, which had been purloined by his grandfather in 1296, and the return of which had also been agreed upon in the terms of the Edinburgh – Northampton treaty of 1328! The treaty had stated as well that Scotland would be recognised by England as a fully independent country, the recognised rulers of which were to be King Robert I (the Bruce) and his heirs and successors, and the border of which would be as that recognised under King Alexander III in 1286 which was roughly as it is today – on a line from the Solway Firth in the west to Berwick upon Tweed in the east. All this was due to cost Scotland a trifling £100,000 in sterling! More importantly, it also negated the Treaty of Abernethy of 1072!

The English in general and Edward in particular, supported the 49 year old Edward Balliol in his invasion of Scotland and defeat of the Scots, who were led by the guardian, Donald Earl of Mar, at the Battle of Duppin in Perthshire on the 12th of August 1332. Mar had only just replaced Moray as guardian 10 days previously after Moray's demise on the 20th of July 1332, and unfortunately, met his own demise during this battle! Mar, in his turn, was replaced by Sir Andrew Murray, Lord of Bothwell, and a brother-in-law of Robert the Bruce, who was unfortunately taken prisoner at Roxburgh in April 1333 and was, in his turn, replaced by Archibald Douglas who proceeded to get himself killed at the Battle of Halidon Hill in the July of that year! Sir Andrew Murray was re-elected as guardian after his release in 1335 and held it up to his death in 1338.

Balliol subsequently had himself crowned de facto King of Scots at Scone on the 24th of September 1332, a month after the Battle of Duppin. Three months later however, he was forced to flee back to England following a surprise attack by nobles loyal to David II at the Battle of Annan. On the 19th of July 1333 however, he and his English supporters were once again victorious and Balliol was restored after the battle of Halidon Hill. At this point the nine year old David and his wife Joan fled to Dumbarton Castle en-route to an eight year refuge in France for his own safe-keeping. It must be remembered here that the death of Robert the Bruce had weakened Scotland considerably since his son David was still a child, and his two most able lieutenants, Sir James, Lord of Douglas (aka the Black Douglas) and Thomas Randolph, 1st Earl of Moray, had both died shortly after himself.

During much of David's absence, the struggle between his current guardian, Sir Andrew Murray and Edward Balliol, still supported by Edward, continually ebbed and flowed until Balliol was finally chased from the field by Murray in 1337 when he (Balliol) discovered that his mentor Edward was now more interested in war with France than supporting any more pointless and expensive expeditions northwards in support of Balliol's pretentious claim to the Scottish throne! David, now seventeen, returned from France in June 1341 and proceeded to take personal control of the Country. In 1346 he invaded England in support of France and the "Auld Alliance" and promptly lost the Battle of Neville' Cross on the 17th October, getting himself wounded and taken prisoner in the process!

David was held at various places in France and England, including the Tower of London, for the next 11 years until his negotiated release, at a reputed ransom of 100,000 merks, on the 3rd of October 1357 and during which time the Country was ruled by his nephew and heir, Robert the Steward who was the Bruce's daughter Marjorie's son. There is no direct comparison between the medieval "merk" and today's currency but suffice to say 100,000 of them then would be worth many, many millions today, possibly up to a hundred or more! This extortionate sum was payable in instalments and due to the very heavy levels of taxation imposed to provide it, Scotland as a whole quickly sank into abject poverty. Also in 1357 comes the first surviving record of a mention of the "Three Estates" of the Parliament of Scotland; these were made up of the Clergy, the nobility and the towns commissioners and this format remained until prorogued sine die in 1707 with the acts of the union which created the United Kingdom (and Parliament) of Great Britain!

David's incarceration in England from 1346 to 1357 was probably a blessing in disguise, at least for him personally as the plague, the "black death", swept Scotland in 1349 causing a prolific loss of life over the next two years; approximately one third of the entire population of the country died in that period! Initially, this had a brighter side as workers were now in short supply and could bargain for better pay and conditions, as wages rose, prices fell, as traders now had fewer customers to sell to. Repeated attacks of the plague however, coupled with the high costs of wars and high taxes to pay for royal ransoms, quickly brought on economic crises and before too long, the price of food had trebled and the population now faced hunger and homelessness as well as disease!

By 1363 it had become next to impossible to raise David's ransom instalments and he now infuriated all and sundry on two separate counts. Firstly there were strong suggestions, and suspicions, that he was using the taxes raised for the ransom for his own ends and secondly, sought to get rid of this liability by bequeathing Scotland, en bloc, to Edward III or one of his sons, in the full knowledge that Scotland would never accept such an arrangement. In 1364 the Scottish parliament indignantly rejected a proposal, no doubt hatched from the subterfuge, skulduggery and downright treachery of David and Edward by which, Lionel; Duke of Clarence should be declared heir to the throne of Scotland!

Thus, in a few short years, the son, whether intentionally or unwittingly, had done his best to undo the lifetime's work of his father! He even went as far as an attempted agreement with Edward III that if he died childless, the King of England should succeed to the Scottish throne! The Scottish parliament however, refused to ratify this and when David did indeed die childless, despite a second marriage to try and rectify the problem, he was succeeded by his nephew and rightful Heir, Robert the Steward who became King Robert II, grandson of Robert the Bruce and the first of the monarchs in the long lived and far reaching dynasty of the Royal House of Stewart!

To be fair, as was said at the start of this chapter, the man never really had a chance. Son of the Bruce, crowned and married by age 4, exiled in France between the ages of 9 and 17, in captivity in England between the ages of 22 and 33 and influenced by several different guardians in between; it's hardly surprising he struggled to come to terms with his birthright! Despite all this, he did govern with surprising vigour for the last few years of his reign, dealing firmly with recalcitrant nobility and some wider baronial revolts. He also pursued his goal of a lasting peace with England and by the time of his death, the monarchy was stronger, and the Royal finances more prosperous, than might have seemed possible a few years previously. David II died at Edinburgh Castle, suddenly, on the 22nd of February 1371 and was subsequently buried in Holyrood Abbey. He was only the second but also the last, ruler of the House of Bruce.

Footnote about the Stone of Destiny.

The "Stone of Destiny" or "Stone of Scone", sometimes referred to in England as the "Coronation Stone", is an oblong block of red sandstone weighing some three hundredweights and with an iron ring at each end, which was used for centuries in the coronations of monarchs of Scotland and later of England, Great Britain and the United Kingdom. Historically, it was kept at Scone Abbey near Perth and is also known as "Jacob's Pillow", it was last used in the coronation of Elizabeth II in 1953!

The stone, the origins of which are lost forever in the mists of time and are subject to several legends, was stolen by Edward I and taken to Westminster Abbey in 1296 and has since been proven by geologists to have been quarried in the vicinity of Scone, which effectively scotches all the rumour and speculation of its origins being in the Holy Land or Ireland. This also raises the question however, was it was the real stone that Edward stole in the first place, or was it a replica put in place by the monks before the arrival of the English raiders? Edward had the stone, real or fake, fitted into a chair on which most subsequent English monarchs have been crowned, doubtless by this symbolizing his claim to be "Lord Paramount" of Scotland. The Edinburgh – Northampton treaty of 1328 made allowance for its return to Scotland but this agreement was ignored by Edward III so it remained in Westminster for another 600 years.

Through the course of time, James VI of Scotland came to the English throne as James I of England and for the next century or so, the Stewart Kings and Queens of Scotland once again sat on the stone but as their coronation of Kings and Queens of England! It was decided in 1996 that the stone should be returned to Scotland and kept there, only returning to Westminster for coronations. It was returned on the 15th of November 1996 (St. Andrews Day) in a handover ceremony at the border of the two Countries, possibly at Carter Bar on the A68, but more probably on the A1 just north of Berwick upon Tweed. The handover was between representatives of the Home Office and the Scottish Office and it was then transported to Edinburgh Castle where it remains to this day in the crown room along with the Crown Jewels and other Regalia of Scotland.

A Chronological Glossary of the Stewart Dynasty

After some possibly cumbersome but nonetheless relevant preliminaries involving Interregnums, Balliol, the Bruce's, the Plantagenet's and the Comyns, not to mention Bannockburn, we arrive at last at the purpose of this book, The House of Stewart! I decided, albeit in hindsight, at this point to insert a glossary as a quick reference point with all the necessary dates and other important data to hand. Basically, the dynasty suffered from two fundamental problems, the first being, for one reason or another, minority reigns! For something like a total of 72 years, between 1406 and 1583, seven successive Stewart monarchs had to begin their reigns under the direct influence of regents or governors and for various lengths of time, from between a couple of years to eighteen years. This obviously created untold mayhem in the ranks of the nobility as they jostled for positions of power under each successive monarch! The second blight on them was Religion! This first reared its ugly head in the reign of Mary Queen of Scots and got progressively and relentlessly more troublesome from then on, ad-infinitum! Both these problems are dealt with in more detail as we progress monarch by monarch through the dynasty.

King Robert II. Born on 2/3/1316, Reigned 22/2/1371 – 19/4/1390, crowned 26/3/1371, Died naturally on 19/4/1390.

King Robert III. Born on 14/8/1337 as John, Reigned 19/4 1390 – 4/4/1406 as Robert, crowned 14/8/1390, Died naturally on 4/4/1406.

King James I. Born 25/7/1394, Reigned 4/4/1406 – 21/2/1437, crowned 21/5/1424, Died 21/2/1437. He was murdered in Blackfriars Monastery, Perth.

King James II. Born 16/10/1430, Reigned 21/2/1437 – 3/8/1460, crowned 25/3/1437, Died 3/8/1460. He was killed by a cannon exploding.

King James III. Born 10/7/1451, Reigned 3/8/1460 – 11/6/1488, crowned 10/8/1460, Died 11/6/1488. It is unsure whether James was murdered or died in battle.

King James IV. Born 17/3/1473, Reigned 11/6/1488 – 9/9/1513, crowned 24/6/1488, Died 9/9/1523. He was killed at the Battle of Flodden.

King James V. Born 10/4/1512, Reigned 9/9/1513 – 14/12/1542, crowned 21/9/1513, Died 14/12/1542. He died of illness on 14/12/1542.

Queen Mary I. Born 7/12/1542, Reigned 14/12/1542 – 24/7/1567, crowned 9/9/1543, Executed 8/2/1587 and known as Mary, Queen of Scots.

King James VI. Born on 19/6/1566, Reigned 24/7/1567 & 24/3/1603 – 27/3/1625, crowned 29/7/1567 & 25/7/1603, Died naturally on 27/3/1625.

King Charles I. Born on 19/11/1600, Reigned 27/3/1625 – 30/1/1649, crowned 18/6/1633 & 2/2/1626, Executed on 30/1/1649.

King Charles II. Born on 29/5/1630, Reigned 30/1/1649 & 29/5/1660 – 6/2/1685, crowned 1/1/1651 & 23/5/1661. He died of illness on 6/2/1685.

King James VII. Born on 14/10/1633, Reigned 6/2/1685 – 11/12/1688, crowned 23/4/1685,

Died in exile on 16/9/1701. Abdicated / exiled in 1689.

King William III, Queen Mary II.   Dual monarchs! William was born on 4/11/1650 & Mary on 30/4/1662, both ascended the throne on 13/2/1689 and both were crowned on 11/4/1689.   Mary died on 28/12/1694 of smallpox & William on 8/3/1702 of pneumonia.

Queen Anne Born on 6/2/1665, Reigned 8/3/1702 – 1/8/1714, crowned 23/4/1702, Died 1/8/1714.   Anne died from the effects of an earlier, severe stroke.

Where dual dates are quoted in the cases of James VI, Charles I and Charles II, the first mentioned dates are relevant to Scotland and the second ones to England and / or Britain. This anomaly is due to the occurrence of the Union of the Crowns in 1603 during the reign of James VI and the subsequent upheaval thereafter. Take James VI for example, he reigned in Scotland from1567 to 1625 but in England his reign only began 1603! He was crowned in Scotland in 1567 but not in England until 1603. The cases of Charles I and Charles II are a bit more complicated and will be explained in further detail in the relevant chapters later on!

Robert Stewart, King Robert II, 1371-1390

Now at last, after some substantial but necessary, and I hope enlightening, groundwork we arrive at the Stewarts proper, albeit the early ones, with Robert II, grandson of Robert the Bruce, courtesy of his daughter Marjorie and her husband Walter Stewart, 6th High Steward of Scotland! Robert chose to follow tradition and be known by his father's surname thus becoming the first in a long line of monarchs from the Royal House of Stewart; otherwise he would have been the third monarch of the House of Bruce and who knows, history may have panned out differently! Born on the 2nd of March 1316 Robert was 55 years of age, and by medieval standards an old man, when he was crowned on the 26th of March 1371 at Scone Abbey, inheriting the throne 32 days earlier on the death of his nephew, King David II who was eight years his junior.

Much earlier, at the age of ten, he had also inherited the title of 7th High Steward of Scotland on his father's death on the 9th of April 1326. This was an ancient title dating back to his Norman ancestor and the first holder; Walter Fitzalan in 1150. The name was changed to Stewart by his grandson in 1204 and the title of High Steward was eventually merged with the title of the Dukes of Rothesay - which is the capital town on the island of Bute - in 1398 and where it remains to the present day with our own Prince Charles. This lineage is the most senior branch of the clan and became known as the Appin or Royal Stewarts. As the name and title suggests, their lands are bordered by Loch Linnhe to the north, Loch Lomond to the west, the river Clyde to the south and takes in the Mull of Kintyre and the islands of Bute, Mull, Islay, Jura, Colonsay, Coll and Tiree.

Heir presumptive for more than fifty years, Robert II had had little effect on Scottish political or military affairs when he finally acceded to the throne in 1371. From October 1318, on the death of his grand-uncle Edward Bruce at the battle of Dundalk in Ireland, he had been heir presumptive to his maternal grandfather, Robert the Bruce, but lost this position upon the birth of his nephew, Bruce's son David by his second wife Elizabeth De Burgh, in 1324. The position was restored however, two years later when Robert was ten, by a parliament at Cambuskenneth when they confirmed him as heir apparent to David II should that Monarch die without issue. The reinstatement of this status was accompanied by the gifts of lands in Argyll, Roxburghshire and the Lothian's which greatly extended the Stewart's sphere of influence out with their hereditary stamping grounds of Appin.

Aged only seventeen, Robert took part in the Battle of Halidon Hill on July 10th 1333 where an army led by the English backed pretender, Edward Balliol, and made up of English troops plus Scottish nobles disinherited by Robert the Bruce, were victorious for the second time in two years. Robert's uncle and former guardian, Sir James Stewart, died in this confrontation. When the young King David had escaped to France in May 1334, he had left Robert and John Randolph, the 3rd Earl of Moray, as joint guardians of the Kingdom. Robert's guardianship was removed in September 1335 when it looked as though the Bruce resistance to Balliol was verging on collapse and was transferred to Sir Andrew Murray, Lord of Bothwell. Robert however was re-appointed, aged twenty two in 1338 on the death of Murray and held the post from then until the return of King David from France in June 1341.

Murray had emerged as a potent war leader at the Battle of Culblean on the 30th of November 1335 where he won a decisive victory over an Anglo-Scottish force commanded by David Strathbogie, titular Earl of Atholl and a leading supporter of Balliol. Murray was also a real thorn in the side of the English and eventually his campaigns put paid to any chance of Edward III gaining, far less holding, full control over the south of Scotland. Balliol now began to lose many of his supporters to the Bruce / Stewart side as garrisons began to fall. In 1338 however, Robert was re-appointed to the guardian's role on the death of Murray and retained the office until his nephew David's return from France in 1341. Five years later Robert accompanied David into battle at Neville's Cross on the 17th of October 1346 where they not only suffered another defeat, but the King was captured and subsequently ransomed for a totally exorbitant sum. Robert managed to escape the field here unscathed with a compatriot, Patrick, Earl of Dunbar or March, who had commanded the Scottish right flank during the battle.

On the domestic front, aged thirty two, Robert decided it was time to legalise things and married Elizabeth Mure, his long-time partner, sometime around 1348 thereby legitimizing their four sons and six daughters! Elizabeth had previously been Robert's mistress and doubts over the legality of their marriage had led to family disputes over their children's right to succession. The waters were muddied further after her death and Robert's second marriage to Euphemia de Ross in 1355 which produced a further two sons and two daughters. A superior claim was asserted by Euphemia on behalf of her four children and because of this ongoing dispute, her second son Walter, Earl of Atholl was to be instigational in the murder of King James I, grandson of Robert II and Elizabeth Mure in 1437. The line of succession was eventually settled on Elizabeth's and Robert's first born son John, on the 27th of March 1371 by a parliament at Scone Abbey who declared the Lord John, Earl of Carrick and High Steward of Scotland, heir to the Crown.

Some parts of the Lothian's and southern Scotland were still under a bit of English influence at this point, so Robert allowed, and indeed encouraged, his southern Earls to engage in forays into these zones to regain their territories. He also halted trade with England and renewed treaties with France and by 1384, the Scots had re-taken most of these occupied lands. Robert also relinquished the control of the country in this year, first of all to his eldest son John, the future King Robert III, and then from 1388 to John's younger brother Robert, the future and first Duke of Albany, both of whom, in their turn, administered the country's affairs whilst acting as their father's Lieutenants.

Robert, Duke of Albany, third son of Robert II and Elizabeth Mure (their second son Walter, Earl of Fife had died young at 24 years of age in late 1362) was a larger than life character, sadly though, for mostly the wrong reasons. He served as regent, albeit partially in some cases, to three different and successive monarchs, Robert II, Robert III and James I. In addition to his 1398 creation of the first Duke of Albany, he also held the titles of Earl of Mentieth from 28/2/1361, Earl of Fife 1362 - 1372, Earl of Buchan 1394 - 1406 and Earl of Atholl in 1403, but for the duration of Robert III's life only. A totally ruthless politician, he was widely regarded as being responsible for the suspicious death of his nephew David, Duke of Rothesay and brother of the future King James I who, unfortunately spent the first eighteen years of his ascension in captivity in England.

This almost welcome captivity was due in no small part to concern for the young heir's life as the nobles feared that Albany, though exonerated from the murder of David, would also despatch James, given half a chance. James was captured on the 22nd March 1406 by English pirates on his way to France and safety. He was then delivered up to the Court of Henry IV where he spent the next eighteen years of his life in captivity. He succeeded to the throne at the start of this captivity on the death of his father Robert III on the 4th of April 1406, but had to wait until the 21st of May 1424 for his Coronation after he was freed by a ransom payment of forty thousand pounds.

Unlike his predecessor and nephew, David II, who died without issue, Robert seems to have mounted a one man crusade to re-populate, if not the earth, then certainly at least the Scottish part of it! It's hardly surprising that he didn't have a great effect on Scottish political or military matters after his accession in 1371 as he must have been virtually worn out from conducting his own personal stud farm! Apart from his fourteen children from the two legally recognized marriages, he is also credited with the parentage of numerous other offspring by various mistresses in other illicit assignations and affairs!

Under Robert II, the Stewarts greatly increased their holdings all over Scotland, particularly in the west and the North. Apart from the prolific lands and titles granted to his third son, Robert, which were Duke of Albany – Earl of Fife – Earl of Menteith and keeper of Stirling Castle; his first son and heir, John, Earl of Carrick, became the keeper of Edinburgh Castle; his fourth son Alexander got the Earldoms of Buchan and Ross along with the Lordship of Badenoch and also became the King's Justiciar and Lieutenant in the north. David, his eldest son by his second marriage got the Earldoms of Strathearn and Caithness, while Walter, his second son by this marriage became the first Earl of Atholl of the seventh creation of the title. Significantly, Robert's sons-in-law were John McDonald, Lord of the Isles, John Dunbar, Earl of Moray and James Douglas who would become the second Earl of Douglas. Robert's style of Kingship was very different from his predecessor's in that where David had tried to dominate his nobles, Robert's strategy was to subtly delegate authority via his powerful sons and sons-in-law! This worked well as he ended up with influence over eight of the fifteen Earldoms in the country!

In 1373, the third year of his reign, Robert ensured the future of the Stewart dynasty by instructing Parliament to pass certain legislations regarding the succession. At this time none of his sons had heirs so a system had to be devised whereby it could be precisely defined! A totally different problem from his predecessor David! The circumstances under which this could happen, where each of them could inherit the crown but none of which would take precedence over normal succession by Primogeniture were laid down! The country's finances stabilized and indeed, began to flourish during Robert's reign in the seventies and early eighties partly due, amongst other things, to the halting of his predecessor's exorbitant ransom with the demise of Edward III who died of a stroke at Sheen on the 21st of June 1377. Again unlike his predecessor, Robert didn't confine his attentions to a single area of his Kingdom, the south, but often visited the more northern and remote parts as well, among his Gaelic Lords.

By 1384 Robert's son and heir John, Earl of Carrick, had become the foremost Stewart magnate south of the river Forth just as his fourth son Alexander, the Earl of Buchan (aka the wolf of Badenoch) had become so in the north. These two, along with Robert's second surviving son and a future Prince regent, the Earl of Fife, virtually shared a powerbase between them until Robert's death in 1390. In 1388 however, the powerbase shifted from Carrick to Fife with the death of Carrick's close friend and ally, James, Earl of Douglas at the Scottish victory over the English at the Battle of Otterburn in the August of that year. Unfortunately, James had died without an heir and this led to Archibald becoming the new Earl of Douglas. Archibald then switched the Douglas support from the Carrick to the Fife (future Duke of Albany) camp.

Many of the Scottish nobles approved of Fife's declared intention to deal with the lawlessness being perpetrated in the north by his younger brother Alexander. Fife eventually relieved him of his offices of Lieutenant of the north and Justiciar of the Realm north of the Forth. These roles he presented to his own son and the future 2nd Duke of Albany, Murdoch Stewart. Robert II made what was to be a final tour of the north in January 1390 and from which he returned to Dundonald Castle in Ayrshire in the March. He died there on the 19th of April and was buried at Scone on the 25th of April in that same year of 1390.

As a fitting epitaph, it would probably be fair to say that King Robert II, the first of the Stewart Dynasty, did as much, if not more, to secure the future of that Dynasty by his prolific performances in the bed chamber, than he ever did in the chambers of politics or on any of the many battlefields during his nineteen year reign!

John Stewart, King Robert III, 1390-1406

This, the second in the lineage of the early dynasty, brings us to King Robert II's eldest son by his first marriage and heir, John, Earl of Carrick, who changed his name on his accession to the throne in 1390 to Robert, as he believed that King John Balliol had sullied the name "John" by his weak and despicable behaviour during his short reign in capitulating to Edward I's every whim. He was born on the 14th of August 1337 at Scone Palace and was crowned at Scone Abbey on the same date in 1390, fifty three years later. He died as something of a recluse on the 4th of April 1406 in the clan stronghold of Rothesay Castle on Bute and had three sons, by his wife Anabella Drummond. Robert, who died in infancy, David, the future Duke of Rothesay whose death the King's younger brother Robert, Earl of Fife and future Duke of Albany was strongly suspected of, and James, the future James I of Scotland.

John, then styled Lord of Kyle, first appeared in the 1350's as the commander of a campaign in the lordship of Annandale to re-establish Scottish control over English occupied territories. He joined with his father, then Robert the Steward, along with the Earls of Douglas and March in a failed insurrection against his grand-uncle, King David II early in 1363 but had re-submitted to him again shortly afterwards. David both imprisoned John for this for a short spell then made him Earl of Carrick in 1368, he had already been created Earl of Atholl in 1367. His father became King in 1371 with the unexpected death of David and John became influential in the government of the Kingdom in the succeeding years but became impatient at his father's longevity. He was appointed the King's Lieutenant in 1384 having manipulated the general council to remove Robert II from direct rule. By 1388 however, John had been badly incapacitated physically by a horse kick and politically by the loss of his powerful ally James, Earl of Douglas at the Battle of Otterburn. This saw a fundamental swing in the support of the nobility from himself to his younger brother Robert, the Earl of Fife and the future Duke of Albany. This resulted in the council transferring the Lieutenancy from Carrick to Fife in the December of that year of 1388.

Before his ascension he had been known as John, Earl of Carrick, a non-heritable title created in 1186 and which reverted to the crown on either the death of the holder or the holder becoming King. This Earldom was to merge by an act of parliament in 1469 with the Dukedom of Rothesay, a heritable title created in 1398, one presumes by Robert III, and first held by his eldest surviving son, David; it passed to David's younger brother, the future James I of Scotland, upon his (David's) highly suspicious death at the hands of his uncle Robert, Earl of Menteith and Fife and future Duke of Albany, a title relating to Scotland north of the Forth, created in 1398 by his brother the King and of which he was the first holder. The Dukedoms of Rothesay and Albany were the first such titles ever created in Scotland. The Dukedom of Rothesay not only incorporates the Earldom of Carrick but also the "Lordship of the Isles" (since 1493) and "Prince and Great Steward of Scotland" (since 1371)! All of which are held today by our own Prince Charles; Prince of Wales, and used by him when in Scotland.

Unfortunately, upon his accession, the King's younger brother Robert, Earl of Fife still held the Lieutenancy of the country transferred to him since the Battle of Otterburn in 1388 so King

Robert III lacked the authority to rule directly since Fife held that Lieutenancy until 1393! Power was eventually restored to the King, though in conjunction with his son David in the February of that year. John unfortunately, was one of the less influential Stewart Kings, unwilling or unable to wield his regal powers as he could, and indeed, should have, not a lot unlike his regal predecessor, whom he held in contempt, Balliol!

In 1390 his father died and John ascended the throne as King Robert III. Dominated as he was by his younger brother he lacked the authority to rule directly however, as Fife retained his Lieutenancy until February 1393. The King was increasingly blamed for his failure to pacify and control the Gaelic areas of the Kingdom in the west and the north, with the result that the general council held in Perth in April 1398 openly criticised him and empowered his brother and his son, Albany and Rothesay respectively, who were the first ever Dukes created in Scotland, to lead an army against Donald, Lord of the Isles and his brothers. For whatever reason, this well prepared and equipped expedition came to naught and the Islemen continued on their merry way. Descended as they were from generations of Viking and Gaelic warlords, they wielded their power virtually unopposed throughout the western highlands and islands via fleets of sea-going galleys.

Previous to this, power had been returned to the King but in conjunction with his son David who, six years later, in 1399 and now the Duke of Rothesay became the Lieutenant of the Kingdom in his own right. This though, was under the supervision of a special Parliamentary group dominated by who else but Fife, now the Duke of Albany. After this Robert virtually retired to Rothesay Castle on the Isle of Bute fearing for his own safety as well as that of his son James as a dispute between Albany and Rothesay had resulted in Rothesay being imprisoned in Albany's Falkland Castle where he later died in March 1402 in highly suspicious circumstances, starvation was strongly suspected.

Albany was not only absolved of blame for this by the general counsel but they even re-appointed him to the Lieutenancy of the country! This in spite of the fact that Albany was known to be an ambitious man and that his designs on the throne were also well known. Fearing now for his remaining son's life as well as his own, as they were all that now stood between the ambitious Albany and the crown, Robert arranged for the future James I to flee to

France in early 1406 with the help of a powerful group of followers. This however went awry, and James ended up a prisoner in England and remained so for the next Eighteen years. Robert's heir apparent was captured on the 22nd of March 1406 and Robert himself died two weeks later on the 4th of April 1406 at Rothesay Castle on Bute; he was buried in the Stewart foundation Abbey of Paisley. This resulted in another Scottish King, albeit uncrowned this time, spending many years in captivity in England with yet another ransom having to be organized and paid to secure his release. Shades of his grandfather, David II!

Some historians claim that Robert was never the real ruler of Scotland during his sixteen year reign and apparently he was well aware of his own shortcomings when he allegedly penned his own epitaph with the words "bury me in a midden and say here lays the worst of Kings and the most wretched of men"! Although there was no genetic link between Robert and John Balliol, the similarities and deficiencies in their character make-up was pretty obvious, both were basically weak men who were willing to do just about anything and make almost any sacrifice in order to have a quiet life! In Robert's case, he had been unwilling, or unable, or by a combination of both, to stand up to his strong brother, either for himself or to provide the necessary security and safety for his sons and their subsequent futures! There is a definite similarity in the natures of Robert III, John Balliol and Edward II of England in that they were not bad men, but were just somewhat weak-willed and malleable, no matches really for the strong and determined adversary's which they all found themselves individually pitted against.

James Stewart, King James I, 1406–1437

James, our third monarch of the dynasty was fortunate, or unfortunate, depending on how one chooses to look at it, in that he became the King of Scotland at all. He was born in late July 1394 at Dunfermline Palace in Fife and was the last of three sons to his father King Robert III and his mother Anabella Drummond. Their first-born, Robert, had died in infancy and their second son David, had died in 1402 while holding the title of the Duke of Rothesay; and in highly suspicious circumstances at Falkland Castle in the custody of his uncle, the Duke of Albany. This left third-born James initially as the Heir Apparent - a position he inherited from his dead brother David on the 26th of March 1402 - and secondly as the future King of Scots, which position he ascended to upon his father's death on the 4th of April 1406 and by which time he was already in captivity in England and at the start of an eighteen year detention there!

This unfortunate turn of events had come about because parliament, and his father Robert III, had feared for James's safety after the questionable death of his elder brother whilst in the "care" of the Duke of Albany and plans were made to send him to France. At the start of his journey there in February 1406, James and his entourage were waylaid by James Douglas of Balvenie, a relative of Archibald, the 4th Earl of Douglas who was a confidant of Albany's - and a fellow conspirator in the death of David the Duke of Rothesay - and were obliged to take refuge on the Bass Rock, an islet in the Firth of Forth. After some weeks there, he boarded a vessel from Danzig, the Maryenknyght, which was bound for France but on the 22nd of March, while off the English coast, they were boarded by enterprising buccaneers and James was delivered up to the English Court of Henry IV. Two weeks later the ailing Robert III died and the uncrowned King of Scots began his eighteen year incarceration.

As soon as James was in captivity, the ambitious Albany who, along with Archibald, the Black Douglas, had been absolved of all blame in the death of David, lost no time - or opportunity - to proceed with a total character assassination. First of all he took James's lands under his own control therefore depriving him of any income as well as commandeering the Regalia of his position. He then ensured that James was only referred to thereafter in all written records as "the son of the late King". All This while simultaneously promoting himself from Lieutenant to Governor of the Realm; thereby making himself King in all but name and simultaneously consolidating the power base of the Albany Stewarts!

Meanwhile, Henry IV had treated the young James well, providing him with a good education and seeing that he was ideally placed to observe the English King's methods of political control and rule. James used personal visits from his nobles; along with letters to individuals to maintain some level of visibility in his kingdom. On Henry's death in 1413, his son Henry V immediately ended James's comparative freedom, placing him in the Tower of London along with other Scots prisoners including his cousin, Murdoch Stewart, Albany's son, who had been captured at the Battle of Homildon Hill in 1402. Initially they were held apart but from late 1413 until Murdoch's release in 1415, they were held together in the Tower and latterly at Windsor Castle.

Archibald, the Black Douglas and 4th Earl of Douglas had also been captured at Homildon Hill whilst heavily wounded, which proved a serious setback to the consolidation of the Albany / Douglas power base. The Douglas remained a prisoner of Sir Henry Percy while recovering from his wounds, until released under oath in 1403 to join with Percy and fight in his conspiracy against Henry IV at the Battle of Shrewsbury. Once again the Douglas was on the wrong end of a heavy defeat and this time ended up as a prisoner of the English King. Ransomed in 1408 he returned to his own border lands to resuscitate his long term understanding with the Albany Stewarts.

James's standing at Henry's Court had increased greatly by 1420 and he began to be seen as more of a guest than a hostage. His value to Henry became apparent when he accompanied the English King to France that same year. He also accompanied him in 1421 and where he actually opposed Scottish troops fighting for the French at the siege of Melun: a contingent of these troops was later hung for this as it was seen as treason against their King! On the 31st of August 1422, Henry V died of dysentery in France and James was part of the escort which was charged with escorting the King's body back to London. After this, the regency Council of the infant King Henry VI were inclined to have James released as soon as possible but their attempts to effect this in early 1423 came to naught as the unholy alliance of the Albany Stewarts and the Douglas's were having none of it!

The cunning Douglas however, was playing both sides against the middle by this stage of the proceedings! Despite his complicity with Albany in the murder of James's elder brother, David, in Albany's Castle of Falkland in 1402, the Douglas had still been able to engage with the King in his enforced estrangement at the English Court. Now, In return for James's endorsement of the Douglas's position in the Kingdom, the Earl was able to deliver his affinity to the cause of the King's homecoming. The relationship between Douglas and Murdoch Stewart – now 2nd Duke of Albany since his father's death in 1420 – was under considerable strain and almost certainly compelled Murdoch to agree to a general council in August 1423 where it was agreed that a representation should be sent to England to negotiate James's release as soon as possible.

A ransom treaty of some £40.000 was agreed at Durham on the 28th of March 1424 and to which James attached his own personal seal. The King and his Queen, newly married and escorted by English and Scottish nobles, with due pomp and circumstance, reached Melrose Abbey on the 5th of April to be met by Albany who relinquished his governor's seal of office thereby giving allegiance to his King! For political reasons James chose at this point to ally himself with his uncle Walter Stewart, Earl of Atholl, cousin of Albany and youngest son of King Robert II. Walter however, and for his own reasons, was later to prove a major instigator in the King's assassination at Perth!

This was not altogether a popular re-entry by the King to his realm as first of all, he had raised arms for Henry V against his fellow Scots in France, and secondly, Scots nobles would now have to pay increased taxes to cover the £40,000 ransom, and on top of that, would also have to provide hostages as security! One of these unfortunate hostages was David Stewart the second son of the above mentioned Walter, Earl of Atholl! David subsequently died in captivity in 1434! Contrary to all this however, the King held many qualities that were admired, he excelled at sport and was greatly appreciative of literature and music. Also, unlike his predecessors, he did not take mistresses but had eight children by his consort, Queen Joan. He had married Joan Beaufort, a cousin of Henry VI and the niece of Thomas, Duke of Exeter and Henry, Bishop of Winchester, in the February of 1424. Six of these were girls and only the sixth and seventh children were male: these were in fact twins but the eldest, Alexander died in infancy leaving his younger brother James as the heir apparent to the crown. In the meantime, James's Coronation took place at Scone on the 21st of May 1424.

Initially, the King shied clear from controversy as much as possible as he was still beholden to the nobility – particularly the Douglas's – for support in many areas of governing the country. The exception to this was Walter Stewart, son of Murdoch Stewart, the 2nd Duke of Albany and grandson to the original Duke, Robert, who had been the third son of King Robert II. James had Walter arrested and imprisoned on the Bass Rock on the 13th May 1424 which was probably in Murdoch's interests as well as James's; as he had been in open revolt against his father on private family inheritance matters, as well as with his father's acquiescence to the return of James to Scotland.

James probably felt unable to move against the rest of the Albany Stewarts at this time as Murdoch's brother John Stewart, Earl of Buchan and Archibald, 4th Earl of Douglas were fighting for the Dauphinist cause against the English in France. Both these men however, fell at the Battle of Verneuil in August 1424 where a large Scottish army was routed. This twin misfortune, the loss of his brother as well as a large fighting force, left Murdoch politically exposed and vulnerable.   Archibald, 5th Earl of Douglas's position was also compromised by the death of his father here. All in all, an excellent result for the King!

The King's rancour against the Albany Stewarts was rooted in the past; he held the first Duke, Robert, responsible for his brother David's death and was of the opinion that neither he, nor his son Murdoch, had exerted themselves in any way to obtain his own release from captivity, leading him to suspect that they indeed held aspirations for the throne itself. A parliamentary session in March 1425 precipitated the arrests of Murdoch, his wife Isabella and his son Alexander, Walter was already imprisoned and the youngest son, James – known as James the fat – escaped to lead the men of Lennox and Argyll in open rebellion against the crown by taking the town of Dumbarton and killing the keeper of its castle which gave the King all the ammunition he needed to bring about a charge of treason against the whole clan! James the fat's success though was short-lived and he fled to Ireland where he eventually died in exile! An assize of seven Earls and fourteen lesser nobles heard these charges at Stirling Castle and on the 25th of

May found the defendants guilty as charged, sentencing them to instant death, which was carried out to the letter of the law by beheading them in front of the Castle. That year of 1425, with Murdoch's death, saw the forfeiture of the Dukedom of Albany as it was now considered tainted, it was however, to be recreated again in 1458 with Alexander, 2nd son of James II.

All this yielded James the three forfeited Earldoms of Fife, Menteith and Lennox. Mar, March and Strathearn were to follow due to previous illegalities uncovered by the crown which also ultimately meant the Lordships of Garioch and Badenoch reverting. Still avaricious, James sought to increase his wealth further through taxation and got Parliament to raise a tax aimed at paying off his ransom: £26,000 was raised but only £12,000 got as far as England! A large slice of this anomaly went to the construction of Linlithgow Palace which works continued until James's death in 1437. As well as being responsible for the undoing of the Albany Stewarts, James also vented his spleen by detaining Alexander, 3rd Lord of the Isles in 1428 and arresting Archibald, 5th Earl of Douglas in 1431. George, Earl of March followed suit in 1434.

James's obsession with asserting his authority didn't stop with the nobility; he also endeared himself by inflicting it on the Church, lamenting that his predecessor King David II's benevolence towards it had cost the crown dear over the years. He also sought to bring the Church's attitudes into line with his policies by having his own clerics appointed to the bishoprics of Glasgow, Dunblane, Dunkeld and Moray. He followed this up by having parliament declare in March 1425 that all bishops must instruct their clerics to "offer up prayers for the King and his family". A year later this was extended to insist that "prayers be given at every mass under sanction of a fine and severe rebuke"!

Not content with venting his authoritive bent on the Church and his southern nobility, James now turned his attention to the north and west of his Kingdom! In the hope that he would become a faithful servant of the crown, he granted Alexander, 3rd Lord of the Isles his freedom; whereupon that Lord promptly led a rebellion attacking Inverness in early 1429! This crisis deepened when a fleet was dispatched from the Lordship to bring the now deceased Murdoch, Duke of Albany's youngest son James the fat, back from Ulster to claim the crown. With James's intention to ally himself with the Ulster

O'Donnell's against the McDonalds, the English now became distrustful of the Scottish King and they then tried to bring James the fat to England for similar motives to Alexander's. Before he could become an active player for either side however, James the fat died suddenly, thus releasing the King to prepare for decisive action against the Lordship.

The armies met on June 21st 1429 in Lochaber, and Alexander, due to the defections of the Clans Chattan and Cameron, was heavily defeated. The King pushed home his advantage by dispatching an army, reinforced with artillery to the Isles where Alexander, realising his hopeless position, tried to negotiate terms but James demanded, and received, his total submission. The King then delegated royal authority to Alexander Stewart, Earl of Mar for the keeping of the King's peace in the north and west from August 1429.

The arrest and imprisonment of the 5th Earl of Douglas had also served to increase political tensions and James, now realising this, acted by freeing the Earl on 29th September 1431. He made it a condition of his release however, that Archibald backed the King at the forthcoming parliament where James intended to push for further funds to resuscitate his campaigns against Alexander and the Islemen. Parliament was in no mood to allow James this unconditional backing, he was allowed his tax but parliament retained control of it. This effectively brought to an end James's near persecution of the Highland clans.

On the European stage, James had his clout greatly increased in October 1428 by the proposal of an impending marriage between his eldest daughter, the Princess Margaret then aged four, to Louis the Dauphine of France then aged seven, which carried with it the gift of the province of Saintonge to James, as well as a renewal and strengthening of the Auld Alliance. This marriage eventually took place on 25th June 1436 and in the August Scotland entered the Anglo – Franco war at France's request with James leading a large army, with artillery, to lay siege to the English enclave of Roxburgh Castle. This foray however was doomed to disaster due to mismanagement at the top and disharmony and squabbling at almost every other level! When the militant Prelates of York and Durham, aided and abetted by the Earl of Northumberland, arrived to relive the fortress, the Scots broke and fled, abandoning their expensive artillery pieces to the English. This was a major disaster for James both in terms of foreign policy and internal authority!

It left him open to searching questions regarding his control over his subjects, his military competence and his diplomatic abilities; but in spite of all this he remained determined to maintain hostilities against England. Two months after Roxburgh, In October 1436, James called a general council to finance further aggression through more taxation. This was firmly resisted and was articulated by Sir Robert Graham, a former Albany attendant and now a servant of Atholl. Graham then attempted, unsuccessfully, to arrest the King which resulted in that Knight's imprisonment, followed by banishment, but James failed to see this as part of any extended threat! Atholl was rebuffed yet again when James overturned the chapter of Dunkeld Cathedral in favour of his nephew and firm supporter, James Kennedy whom he appointed bishop there. He was later transferred to St Andrews in 1440 and was to become the most influential churchman of James II's reign.

There was now a reactionary groundswell of feeling against the King which demonstrated to Atholl that James was not only on the back foot; but was becoming highly unpopular to boot, and that his assassination was now a viable option! It is unclear whether Atholl was deliberately setting the main protagonists against each other to clear his own way to the throne, or if he had a huge resentment at the death of his son David in 1434, in captivity in England as a hostage for James, but whichever, the onetime King's stalwart was now clearly agin' the establishment and in favour of conspiracy and regicide! There was now also much long standing resentment against James for his witch-hunt of the Albany Stewarts in 1425 and this was coming home to roost along with along with all the other recent events such as the total fiasco at Roxburgh. Many saw his treatment of the Albany Stewarts as akin to his great-great-grandfather's persecution of the Comyns in 1308.

A general council was held in Atholl's heartland of Perth on the 4th of February 1437 and fortunately for the conspirators, the King and Queen remained at their town lodgings of the Blackfriars monastery for the duration. In the evening of the 20th of February the Royals were in their rooms and separated from most of their servants when Atholl's grandson and heir, Robert Stewart, also the King's chamberlain, allowed his co-conspirators access to the building. They were thought to number around thirty and were led by Sir Robert Graham: James was alerted to their presence which gave him time to hide in a sewer, but with its exit recently blocked to prevent the loss of tennis balls, James was trapped and killed! His Queen, though wounded, and six year old son, now James II, survived the attempted coup.

It is possible that had the botched attempt on the Queen's life succeeded, and Atholl had taken control of the young King, the eventual outcome would have been very different. As it was, Queen Joan's small group of loyal supporters, which included the Earl of Angus and Lord William Crichton, governor of Edinburgh Castle and Master of the Royal Household, ensured her continued hold of James which greatly reinforced her situation and her claim to the regency. Atholl however, still had followers and neither side could claim the ascendancy so the Pope's envoy, the Bishop of Urbino was called in to arbitrate.

By the middle of March, Atholl on the one side and Angus and Crichton on the other, were at each other's throats but Atholl's position collapsed with the capture of his heir Robert Stewart who confessed the whole sorry business and their parts in it! Walter, Earl of Atholl, was captured and imprisoned at the Edinburgh

Tollbooth where he was tried and eventually beheaded on the 26th of March 1437 after enduring three days of totally hideous and barbaric torture.

Sir Robert Graham, the leader of the band of assassins, was captured and tried at Stirling Castle and duly executed sometime after the 9th of April.

The Queen's pursuit of the regency ended in June 1437 with the appointment of Archibald, 5th Earl of Douglas to act as Lieutenant – General of the Kingdom.

James I was buried at Perth Charterhouse (Perth Priory) and one of his major contributions to history in 1424 was to have the Scottish parliament record their acts in Scots rather than in Latin. He also failed in 1426 in an attempt to make the Scottish parliament more accountable for its actions, much along the lines of its English counterpart.

James Stewart, King James II, 1437-1460

Born on the 16th of October 1430, this, the fourth subject of our chronicle and the second son of James I and his Queen, Joan Beaufort, inherited a somewhat poisoned chalice at six years of age. In common with his father and other Stewarts, James would never have ascended to the throne if an older brother had lived. In his case, the elder brother was his twin, Alexander Duke of Albany, who had died in infancy leaving James as the Duke of Rothesay and heir apparent to the throne. This he duly ascended to on the 21st of February 1437 with the assassination of his father at Perth. His coronation took place on the 25th of March at Holyrood Abbey in Edinburgh which made him the first of the dynasty to be crowned out - with the Abbey of Scone.

James was a politically and singularly successful King who was popular with the commoners, and with whom, like most of the Stewarts, he chose to socialise, both in times of war as well as in peace. He did not inherit his father's taste for literature, but the foundation of the University of Glasgow by Bishop Turnbull during his reign, shows that he actively encouraged learning. This is further backed up by traces of his endowments to St. Salvador's, the new college of Archbishop Kennedy at St, Andrews. The exceptionally brutal murder of William, the 8th Earl of Douglas on the 22nd of February 1452 at Stirling Castle however, leaves a distinct stain on his otherwise reasonable character.

For the first two years of his reign the business of government was taken care of by his first cousin, Archibald, 5th Earl of Douglas as lieutenant – General of the Realm. After Douglas's death however, and with a dearth of substantial Earls in Scotland due to forfeiture, death and inexperience; political power was uneasily shared between William Lord Crichton, now Lord Chancellor of Scotland, and Sir Alexander Livingston of Callander who had possession of the young King as the warden of the stronghold of Stirling Castle. Taking full advantage of these events, Livingston proceeded to place Queen Joan and her new husband, Sir John Stewart, a direct descendant of the High Stewards of Scotland, under house arrest in the Castle in August 1439. They were released on the 4th of September only after formally agreeing to put

James into the custody of the Livingston's, surrendering the Queen's dowry for his maintenance, and publically confessing that Livingston had acted only through his zeal for the safety of the young King!

In the November of 1440 and supposedly in the King's name, an invitation was sent by the Lord Chancellor, Sir William Crichton, to sixteen year old William, the young 6th Earl of Douglas and his eleven year old brother David, to visit and sup with the King at Edinburgh Castle. This they duly accepted and were entertained at the royal table, but during the meal a black bull's head, the symbol of death, was brought in and whereupon the Douglas's were dragged out to Castle Hill, given a mock trial and subsequently beheaded. It is still unclear who else was responsible for this infamous incident, which is known as "the Black Dinner", but Livingston and Buchan are strong suspects. In these days the Earls of Douglas were known as "the Black Douglas's" and the Earls of Angus as "the Red Douglas's"!

Negotiations began in July 1447 for a possible marriage between James and Mary of Guelders who came recommended by her kinsman, Philip the Good and who settled sixty thousand crowns on her as a dowry. These negotiations came to a satisfactory conclusion in September 1448 and the couple were duly married at Holyrood Palace on the 3rd of July 1449, he was nineteen and she was fifteen! They had eight children only six of whom survived into adulthood, their firstborn a son who was unnamed, was born and died the same day on the 19th of May 1450. Their second son, Alexander, Duke of Albany and James's elder twin brother, died in infancy thereby drawing an uncanny parallel in the line of succession. For the third consecutive time, a Stewart was due to inherit a crown he would never have otherwise inherited if an older brother had lived! Their third son, Alexander's younger twin and future James III was born on the 10th of July 1451. The other children; in order, were Mary, Alexander, David, John and Margaret.

Mary of Guelders, daughter of the Duke of Gelderland, also had many royal ancestors among who were King John II of France and John, King of Bohemia and also Count of Luxembourg. Subsequently, the relations between Scotland and Flanders, already healthy under James I, became even closer and consequently, many Flemings in Mary's suite took the decision to remain and settle in Scotland. 1449 was also the year that James reached adulthood but his "active Kingship" varied little from that of his minority due to Douglas and Crichton continuing to dominate the political power; and the King's ability to reign without them remained limited. These two used the King's "coming of age" to oust the Livingston's from the shared government and the young King also took this chance for revenge on them for the brief arrest of his mother ten years previously!

In the autumn of that year, James's revenge escalated when he had Sir Alexander Livingston and other members of his family arrested; and at a parliament in Edinburgh on the 19th of January 1450, Sir Alexander's son, also Alexander and Robert Livingston were tried and executed on Castle Hill. Sir Alexander and other kinsmen were confined in different castles far apart from each other. A single Livingston escaped this witch hunt, James, Alexander's eldest son who was arrested but escaped to the Highlands: he was later restored in 1454 to the office of Chamberlain to which he had been appointed in 1449.

James however, chose not to acquiesce to all these goings-on without argument and between 1451 and 1455 he struggled to free himself from the power of the Douglas's. Attempts to curb their power by raiding their lands took place in

1451, during the absence of William, the 8th Earl of Douglas from Scotland on a pilgrimage to Rome, and culminated in the murder of the said Earl at Stirling Castle on the 22nd of February 1452 after his return. James apparently justified this act by accusing the Earl (probably rightly) of forming a power base with John Macdonald, 11th Earl of Ross and Lord of the Isles, and Alexander Lindsay, the 4th Earl of Crawford. If true, this trio would have created a major, and dangerous, rival to the Royal authority. On Douglas's refusal to break this alliance, James reportedly became incandescent with rage, stabbed the Earl twenty six times and then threw his body out of a window! His court officials, many of whom would rise to predominance in later years and often in former Douglas lands, then joined in the bloodbath by attacking the Earl's body where it lay, one allegedly striking out Douglas's brains with an axe! Apparently, half – measures and self - restraint didn't count for a lot in these days!

The Earl's murder did not end the power of the Douglas's, but rather created a state of intermittent civil war between 1452 and 1455; the main engagements of which were at Brodick on the Isle of Arran, Inverkip in Renfrew and the Battle of Arkinholm at Langholm in Dumfries and

Galloway. James again attempted to seize Douglas lands but his opponents repeatedly forced him to reconsider his options whereby he eventually retuned the lands to Williams' heir, James Douglas, 9th Earl of Douglas and an uneasy truce ensued. James was sailing close to the wind during this period and could realistically have been ousted, but his patronage of lands, titles and offices to allies of the Douglas's, saw them gradually jump ship to the Royal cause. The decisive blow came in May 1455 when James, represented by the Red Douglas, George, 4th Earl of Angus, comprehensively defeated the Black Douglas's at the Battle of Arkinholm at Langholm.

Following this, the Scottish parliament, to whom James had sworn an oath in 1445 not to alter laws without their consent, declared the extensive Douglas lands forfeit and permanently annexed them to the crown. The Earl fled into an extended English exile and James finally had the freedom to govern as he wished. It can be argued that never again would the successors of the House of Stewart face such a powerful challenge to their authority. Combined with the devastation of the Albany Stewarts in his father's reign along with the ruination of the Comyns in his 3G grandfather's reign, this similar undoing of the Black Douglas's now saw complete consolidation of royal power in Scotland!

James II proved to be an active and interventionalist King from now until his death five years later in 1460. He travelled the country extensively though ambitious plans to annexe Orkney, Shetland and the Isle of Man came to naught. He is argued to have originated the highly dubious practise of raising money by selling remissions for serious crimes and it is also argued that some of the unpopular policies of his son James III also originated in the late 1450's. In 1458 an act of parliament commanded the King to modify his behaviour but it is impossible to say how he would have developed from here had he lived longer. Two other acts of parliament were passed during this period of his life, one in 1455, instigated a proper dress code for MP's and the other, in 1458, saw the persecution of the wolf population in Scotland which led to their extinction by the eighteenth century.

During his life, James had enthusiastically encouraged the use of modern artillery which he had used with some success, particularly against the Black Douglas's. He besieged Roxburgh Castle, possibly to avenge his father's earlier humiliation there, with it but things backfired, literally! On the 3rd of August 1460 he was attempting to fire one of these cannons, known as "the Lion" when it exploded and killed him. The Scots carried on with the siege, led by the Red Douglas, 4th Earl of Angus, and the Castle fell a few days later. Once the Castle was captured his widow Mary ordered its destruction. His son became King as James III and Mary acted as regent until her own death three years later.

James Stewart, King James III, 1460 – 1488

There appears to be some considerable dubiety surrounding the date and venue of this, the fifth incumbent of the dynasty, James III's birth, ranging from July '51 to May '52 and occurring at either Stirling Castle or the Castle of St Andrews. For simplicity's sake, we will go with the 10th of July at Stirling Castle. He succeeded his father, James II, on the 3rd of August 1460 and reigned until his death at, or just after, the Battle of Sauchieburn on the 11th of June 1488. Unfortunately, there appears to be as much dubiety surrounding his death as there was concerning his birth, this man seems to have been a truly enigmatic person in many different ways! His coronation took place on the 10th of August 1460 at Kelso Abbey which was close to where his father had been killed at Roxburgh Castle; this was organised by his mother, Mary of Guelders, who, for whatever reason, treated the situation as a matter of haste and not a little urgency.

Mary acted as regent for her son until her own death in 1463 and during which time briefly secured the return of Berwick upon Tweed to Scotland. This came about in the form of a gratuity from Margaret of Anjou on behalf of her husband, Henry VI of England in return for Mary's help against the Yorkists in the Wars of the Roses. From 1463 to 1466 the Kennedy's, bishop James of St Andrews and his brother Lord Gilbert, were in charge of the young King's governmental affairs. They in turn were succeeded by Robert, Lord Boyd until 1469 when James turned eighteen and the unscrupulous Boyd had fled the country to Alnwick in Northumberland. Robert, who was aided and abetted by his equally unscrupulous brother, Sir Alexander Boyd, forcibly assumed guardianship of the underage King in 1466 which was a familiar, but dangerous route to power in medieval Scotland!

Between them they managed to underestimate the dangers of this while overestimating their support and the inevitable happened. Before that though, Robert oversaw the cession of the Orkney and Shetland Isles to Scotland on the 8th of September 1468 from the King of Denmark, Norway and Sweden, Christian I, and for whose daughter, Margaret of Denmark, he had arranged marriage with James III. This took place on the 13th of July 1469 at Holyrood Abbey in Edinburgh and their union produced three sons, James IV of Scotland in 1473, James Stewart, Duke of Ross in 1476 and John Stewart, Earl of Mar in 1479. It was suggested at the time that when the younger James was born, the elder one was seriously ill and not expected to survive, hence the two James's but there is no actual proof of this, another unclear and questionable situation in this man's life! Apparently though, it was not an uncommon practise in medieval Scotland to have two sons, or even three, in the one family with the same Christian name, one can only imagine the horrendous confusions and misunderstandings that this must have led to!

Robert Boyd however, had made a momentous and fatal mistake in arranging another marriage in 1467; that of his son Thomas, who was created Earl of Arran for the occasion and Mary, the elder sister of James III. This aroused the jealousy of the other nobles and enraged the King who saw it as an unforgivable insult! Suffice to say Boyd's days were numbered and Mary's marriage to his son was later declared void in 1473. Broadly speaking, James was a pretty unpopular and ineffective monarch after his "coming of age"; many in fact, apparently preferred his wife Margaret as a monarch. This was mainly due to reluctance to face up to his responsibilities, pursuing a policy of friendship with England and disastrous relationships with most of his immediate and extended family. He was also often criticised for his "unmanly" preferences for music etc as opposed to hunting and war-mongering. In 1471 parliament passed an act banning football and golf in favour of the practice of archery in preparation for any future hostilities!

The King's policies in the 1470's consisted of ambitious schemes for territorial expansion such as proposals to invade or annexe the likes of Brittany or Guelders by firstly forming an alliance with England; needless to say, these were laughed out of court. In 1474 he launched an abortive attempt at a marriage alliance between his son and heir, the one year old James, and Cecily of York, a much more mature five year old and the daughter of Edward IV and Elizabeth Woodville! This also proved to be not only unpopular but was greeted with something like contempt! Conflicts developed during this decade as well between the King and his brothers, Alexander, first incumbent of the second creation of the Dukedom of Albany and John, the Earl of Mar. Mar was accused of treason and imprisoned at Craigmiller Castle, near Edinburgh. He died in suspicious circumstances in 1479, probably on the orders of his brother James. His estates and titles were forfeit, and it is thought that James presented the estates to a low-born "favourite" of his, one Robert Cochrane. Albany, also accused of treason, fled to France the same year, once again allowing the Albany title to lapse into forfeiture.

By the end of the decade and into the early 1480's the situation between Scotland and England, or more precisely between James III and Edward IV, had degenerated into a state of sporadic warfare. In 1482 Edward IV launched a full scale invasion force led by his brother Richard, the Duke of Gloucester and future King Richard III, who was aided and abetted by a Duke of Albany who had been reinstated by his brother James in an attempt at reconciliation but which obviously failed dismally! They marched at the head of one of the biggest English armies assembled since the Scottish Wars of Independence, to Berwick, which was seized for the final time, and then on to Edinburgh with a smaller force. James attempted to lead his subjects against the invasion in the July of that year but was arrested by a group of disaffected nobles who were suspected of being in league with Albany, at Lauder and was subsequently imprisoned in Edinburgh Castle. A new regime, led by the self-styled "Lieutenant – General" Albany became established during the autumn of '82 but at the same time, lost the support of the English who, unable to take Edinburgh Castle and running out of money, upped-sticks and headed for home!

With the English gone, the King was able to regain power by buying off members of Albany's short lived government and by the December of '82, that government was collapsing. Albany's attempt to claim the vacant Earldom of Mar for himself also led to the intervention, on the King's side, of the enraged and very powerful, George Gordon 2nd Earl of Huntley who, if truth be known, wanted that particular cherry for himself! All this resulted in Albany's flight to his estates at Dunbar at the Yuletide of 1482. In January 1483, he made a second, abortive attempt to seize the King but with the death of Edward IV on the 9th of April that year, his position became untenable and he fled to England, leaving the gates of Dunbar Castle open for an English garrison to enter as he went! He now forfeited for the second and final time, his title of Duke of Albany, which was then held in abeyance until 1515 when his son John inherited it. He held it until his death in 1536 when this, the second creation of the title, became extinct.

Not done yet, Alexander invaded once again with a small force in July 1484 and joined forces with James, the 9th Earl of Douglas. This resulted in the Battle of Lochmaben which was a resounding victory for the King's forces, Douglas was captured and Alexander once again fled, to France once more, where he died a year later as a result of an accident during a joust in Paris. The aforementioned Earldom of Mar, so sought after by Albany and forfeited by his brother John in 1479, was in fact bestowed upon his nephew, also John, by the king on the2nd of March1486 and remained with him till his death in 1503.

King James III refused to reform his behaviour despite all the strife and political unrest of the late '70's and early '80's. His obsession of obtaining an alliance with England continued, he carried on with his policy of favouring certain low-born "friends" above his nobles, he still refused to travel to implement justice, and he was now estranged from his wife Margaret as well as his eldest son, favouring his second son instead, all of which led to a steadily deteriorating situation which a lot of people were unhappy with! Persistent rumours had been circulating for some time regarding James's sexuality and other serious controversies, and these recent events, plus his bestowing of an Earldom on his "friend" John Ramsey, did nothing to quell them.

He further exacerbated this precarious situation in January 1488 by trying to gain supporters, first of all elevating his favoured second son James as the Duke of Ross; he had inherited the title of the Earl of Ross in 1481 from John, Lord of the Isles, who had forfeited it to the crown. He then elevated four lairds to full Lords of Parliament; these were John Drummond of Cargill made Lord Drummond – Robert Crichton of Sanquhar made Lord Sanquhar – John Hay of Yester made Lord Yester and the Knight William Ruthven made Lord Ruthven. Strong opposition to this was mounted by the Earls of Angus and Argyll as well as by the powerful Home and Hepburn families. The King's eldest son and heir became the figurehead of this opposition party, whether this was with reluctance or possibly provoked by the favouritism being shown by his father to his younger brother is not clear. The result of it all was the King's death at the Battle of Sauchieburn on the 11th of June 1488.

How exactly the King's death came about is still not clear and is clothed by rumour and speculation. Several stories abound and none of

126

them can be proved or disproved. One is that he was killed in the heat of the battle; another has his horse throwing him and trampling him to death sometime around the time of the battle and a third has him fleeing the battle only to be assassinated by a mysterious person dressed as a priest! The general consensus of opinion agrees that it is probably unfair, considering that he actively pursued military conflict several times in his life, to label him a coward and fleeing the scene, so he has been given the benefit of the doubt by dying an honourable death in battle! An enigmatic and controversial man to the end, in many different ways! James was buried at Cambuskenneth Abbey, near Stirling, along with the remains of his wife Margaret who had predeceased him on the 14th of July 1486.

James Stewart, King James IV, 1488 – 1513

King James IV of Scotland first saw the cold light of day on the 17th of March 1473 courtesy of his father James III and his mother Margaret of Denmark, under the arrangements of whose wedding dowry, the Orkney and Shetland Islands were ceded from Scandinavian rule to Scotland. He ascended to the Throne on the 11th of June 1488 at the tender age of just fifteen, after his father's death at the Battle of Sauchieburn which had been orchestrated by a section of the Scottish nobility, as they became increasingly dissatisfied with James's weaknesses and alleged bisexuality. Things had come to a head when James III conferred an Earldom on his "friend" John Ramsey and the nobles called for his son to be proclaimed King in his stead. His son had probably been an unwilling participant in these events but even so, chose to wear an iron belt, or cilice, around his waist next to the skin, ad infinitum, in penance for this and added extra ounces in weight to it each year at Lent!

This James was the twelfth great-grandfather of our present Monarch, Queen Elizabeth II, was also the sixth successive Monarch of the House of Stewart and the fifth great-grandson of King Robert the Bruce! His Coronation took place on the 26th of June 1488 at Scone Abbey and he was destined to die at the major Scottish disaster on Flodden Field in 1513 at the age of forty and after which it is presumed his body was taken to London and is buried either at the Church of Saint Michael or at Sheen Abbey, Surrey! Some dubiety however, is cast upon this account by the fact that the body recovered by the English from the field of battle did not have an iron belt around its waist! The absence of this was explained in some quarters by the possibility of James temporarily discarding it as he dallied with Elizabeth, Lady Heard, at Ford castle prior to proceeding to Flodden. James IV was the last reigning monarch not only of Scotland, but also Great Britain, to be killed in battle! He was also generally regarded as the most successful of the Stewart monarchs in Scotland, being seen as both effective and wise.

After a failed attempt in 1474 by his father to form a wedding alliance with the Princess Cecily of York, Edward IV's daughter, James married his fourth cousin Margaret Tudor, daughter of Henry

VII of England on the 8th of August 1503 after several proxy preliminaries, including a treaty of "Perpetual Peace" signed the year before with his future father-in-law. She was thirteen, he was thirty and their wedding was to ultimately bring about the unification of the two Crowns. They had four sons and two daughters, both of whom were stillborn. The four sons were James, Duke of Rothesay who died in infancy – Arthur, Duke of Rothesay who also died in infancy – James V of Scotland, their only child to reach adulthood and yet another example of a Stewart King who would never have been crowned but for the deaths of older siblings – and Alexander, Duke of Ross who also died in infancy! The King was also known to have fathered several illegitimate children as well so he certainly didn't suffer genetically from his father's supposed sexuality problems!

James dealt effectively with a rebellious section of his nobility early in his reign in 1489, took a direct interest – unlike his father - in the administration of justice in his realm and then finally finished the work started by his forbears by bringing the Lord of the Isles, John MacDonald II to heel in 1493. This was no mean feat as outside of the Kings of Scotland and England, the Lord of the Isles – at their height – was the greatest landowners and most powerful Lords in the British Isles. Since then, that designation, along with the Dukedom of Rothesay, has been held by the eldest son of the reigning Scottish (and later British) monarch. Today they are held by Charles, Prince of Wales. James was instrumental in 1496 of the passing of an act of parliament which made schooling compulsory for the sons of barons and the rich. This was the first "education act" and made the Scottish system one of the best in Europe! We can only wonder at what happened between then and now!

For a while after this, James supported Perkin Warbeck, a pretender to the English throne and even carried out a brief invasion on his behalf in September 1496. Warbeck claimed to be Richard of Shrewsbury, 1st Duke of York and younger son of Edward IV; one of "the Princes in the Tower" and as such, was a significant threat to the foundling Tudor dynasty. Warbeck eventually confessed to his duplicity (under torture?) after his capture and just before he was hanged at Tyburn in November 1499. In August 1497, again one surmises in support of Warbeck, James laid siege to Norham Castle in Northumberland for two weeks, bombarding its walls with heavy artillery which included "Mons

Meg", a 22" calibre cannon which sits today in Edinburgh Castle. Norham was eventually relieved by an English force and its defences rebuilt only to be destroyed again by James sixteen years later on his way to Flodden and subsequent disaster!

James however, didn't fail to recognise that peace between Scotland and England was in the long-term interests of both countries and to this end, ratified the Treaty of Ayton in February 1498 then signed the Treaty of Perpetual Peace with Henry VII in 1502. Jointly, these were supposed to end the state of intermittent warfare which had existed between the two countries for over two hundred years, without any great success though, and which descended into spectacular failure as well as open warfare with James's invasion in 1513! They did however, lead directly to the Union of the Crowns 100 years later with the marriage of Margaret Tudor and James IV in 1503 which also became known as the "joining of the Thistle and the Rose". Despite these agreements however, the canny James also maintained his relations with France and the "Auld Alliance".

The King also realised the importance of maintaining and expanding a strong maritime presence and to that end founded two new dockyards for this purpose, acquiring a total of thirty eight ships for the Royal Scots Navy! These included the "Margaret" and the "Great Michael", this latter was built at great expense at Newhaven, launched in 1511 and was the biggest and most heavily armed ship in Europe at that time! After the disaster of Flodden, the "Great Michael" was sold to France and renamed "Le Grande Nef d'Ecosse" (the big nave, or ship, of Scotland) and is generally believed to have been docked at Brest in 1514 and left there to rot! There is however another train of thought that, under her new name, she took part in the French attack on England in 1545, fighting in the "Battle of the Solent" and the subsequent sinking of the "Mary Rose"!

James was a true Renaissance Prince and interested in practical and scientific matters. He founded the "Royal College of Surgeons", where it is alleged he practised dentistry, in Edinburgh in fifteen hundred and six and a year later established Scotland's first printing press. He added parts to Falkland Palace and the great halls at Edinburgh and Stirling Castles, decorating all of these with tapestries. He was a patron of the arts, well educated and a gifted linguist speaking Latin, French, German, Flemish, Italian and Spanish and was the last King of Scots known to have spoken Gaelic! He was also an accomplished Historian and well read in the Bible and other devout books. James maintained an alchemic workshop with a quintessential furnace at Stirling Castle which consumed quantities of mercury, lead oxide and tin and it is claimed that one of his alchemists, Father Damian, died while attempting to fly from the Castle battlements! There is little wonder that the man thought he could fly, handling these elements on a daily basis!

At the outbreak of war between England and France in October 1511 which was a result of the Italian wars, James found himself in an extremely difficult position as he was an ally by treaty to both of them! When Henry VIII invaded France, James reacted by declaring war on England and received a letter from Pope Leo X on the 28th of June 1513, threatening him with ecclesiastical censure as he had broken his treaty with Henry. He was subsequently excommunicated by Cardinal Bainbridge. Hoping to take advantage of Henry's absence in England while laying siege to Therouanne in France, James led a large and well equipped army south into Northumbria only to die, with many of his Nobles, Clergy and common soldiers at the disastrous battle of Flodden, thoroughly and humiliatingly beaten by a much inferior force! Previously to this he had also sent the Scottish navy, including the Great Michael, south to join the ships of Louis XII of France thereby joining in the "War of the League of Cambrai" which was an ongoing result of the Italian wars and involved most of the European countries eventually!

James decided to use the murder of Robert Kerr, a warden of the Scottish East March in 1508, as a pretext to organise and launch his invasion. Kerr had been killed by one John Heron, known as "the bastard" (a reference to a great cannon of the period and not his legitimacy) and this was used as the catalyst for the Scots to launch an impressive array of both heavy and light infantry, heavy and light cavalry, and also mainly heavy artillery, totalling some 25,000 to 30,000 men at least half of which were destined never to return! The Scots were to lose their King, an Archbishop, two Bishops, eleven Earls, fifteen Lords and three hundred Knights! In effect, a whole generation of the Scottish Nobility was wiped out, to say nothing of about 12,000 men of the rank and file! After the battle was over, many further casualties were sustained by the 15,000 to 20,000 strong non-combatants of the baggage train and camp followers who found themselves undefended and vulnerable on the wrong side of the border!

The Invasion

This began on the 18th of August when the heavy artillery was brought down from Edinburgh Castle to the Netherbow Gate and set off for England, dragged by many oxen. The lighter artillery and the gunners which hadn't sailed with the fleet to France; along with the King and the rest of the army set off the following day, flying the hastily assembled banners of Saint Margaret and Saint Andrew. James had sent notice one month in advance of his intention to invade which was in keeping with his interpretation of the codes of chivalry in force in these days. After a muster on the Burgh Muir of Edinburgh, a spot marked by the "Borestone", which can still be seen today on the left hand side of Morningside Road, a few yards up from Newbattle Terrace heading south; the Scottish host moved on to a campsite north of Duns to await the arrivals of Angus (Archibald Douglas, 5th Earl of Angus) and Home (Alexander Home, 3rd Lord Home).

Their numbers thus swollen by the Douglas's and the cavalry of the Home's, which included the Earl of Huntley's sizeable contingent, the army moved on to ford the river Tweed at Coldstream. By the 29th of August, Norham and Wark Castles had been taken and partly demolished; the Castles of Etal and Ford swiftly fell to the Scots also, giving James control over an eight mile stretch of the river Tweed and the national border! Apparently, prior to this, James wasted some valuable time at Ford Castle in the company of Elizabeth, Lady Heard and her daughter! One story goes that at this point, a small part of the Scottish army returned home while the rest stayed on at Ford waiting for the surrender of Norham and debating their next move. James was itching for a fight and suggested they move against Berwick on Tweed but the Earl of Angus argued against this saying that "they had done enough for France" and was decried for his troubles upon which he returned to Scotland forthwith. His two sons, George Douglas, the Master of Angus and Sir William Douglas of Glenbervie also with the army, both perished with most of their men whilst fighting valiantly in the ensuing battle! Sir William Douglas's wife Elizabeth entered the Convent of St Catherine's of Siena in Edinburgh after her husband's death; the Convent later lent its name to the "Sciennes" area of the city! The last move by the Scots was to fortify positions taken up earlier on the 7th of September at Flodden Edge, which was a strong defensive position, to the south of the village of Branxton! This position was later abandoned due to James's over exaggerated sense of chivalry and fair play, which was expertly manipulated by Surrey!

The Battle

Thomas Howard, Earl of Surrey and commander in chief of King Henry's makeshift home army, hastened north with his numerically much inferior force, outflanking the Scots to the east by crossing the River Till to take up positions to their north and centring on the village of Branxton, which effectively cut off the Scots lines of communication and supply back to Scotland. Surrey, at Wooler on the 7th had complained that Flodden Edge constituted a fortress and challenged James, by asking him to engage in a contract to fight a battle, and meet him on the Friday afternoon on the plain at Millfield, a village three miles North West of Wooler, as arranged! James responded to this by moving his forces from Flodden Edge to a lower ridge at Branxton Hill which still overlooked the English but was two miles away from his original position. This all resulted in the English lined up and facing south and the Scots lined up and facing north! Between the two armies, formed up on their ridges (the Scots being on the higher) lay a valley floor, much of which was damp and even marshy. Hardly the best conditions for a physical battle of the proportions that was to follow, particularly as it was also to involve cavalry!

By eleven o'clock, Surrey's vanguard and artillery had crossed the River Till at the Twizel Bridge. James would not allow his artillery to bombard the English during the execution of this vulnerable manoeuvre as he had agreed with Surrey that actual hostilities would not commence till between midday and three o'clock! The Scots artillery included five Curtals, two Culverins, four Sakers and six Serpentines all heavy and under the charge of one Patrick Painter, the King's secretary. Most of the lighter, more manoeuvrable pieces of the Scots artillery however, were on board the Scottish fleet which was assisting the French against the English and James's brother-in-law Henry VIII. The heavy pieces listed above, had difficulty in lowering their firing angles to target the English on the lower ridge opposite, but the English pieces however, had no such problem and wreaked havoc on the Scottish lines during the opening artillery duel.

It can be argued that James actually lost this battle before it started, and that accusation can be levied at his over-exaggerated sense of Chivalry! In the first place, he allowed Surrey to talk him out of his very strong position at Flodden Edge by the latter's accusation that this constituted "a fortress"! One can only assume that the wily Surrey was probably well aware of James's sense of "fair play" and successfully used it against him here! In the second place, James forbade his heavy ordinance to blast the English to kingdom come during their vulnerable crossing at the Twizel Bridge and thirdly, he had sent most of his lighter ordinance with the fleet to France, therefore denying his army here the use of it! If any one of these situations, particularly the first one, hadn't happened the outcome could have been so very different. If any two of these situations hadn't happened the outcome definitely would have been different and if all three hadn't happened, the English would have been on a hiding to nothing! There again, "if" is a very big word and hindsight is 20/20 vision!

At the start, the Scots were in good order and drawn up in five formations after the textbook German style and made the first move on their left flank with Home and Huntley descending, on their own initiative and without an order from James, to meet the English right flank under the command of Lord Edmund Howard, Surrey's son, and Sir Marmaduke Constable, inflicting considerable damage and casualties on it! The incredible mistake they then made however was to withdraw and rest on their laurels, apparently under the misplaced and totally misguided assumption that the rest of their army would meet with the same easy success which they had just enjoyed!

Spurred on by the success of their left flank, which had taken place on relatively dry ground, the rest of the Scots horde with the exception of their right flank surged down into the valley en-masse and immediately ran into serious problems by getting bogged down in the soft ground! Their centre, led by James and the Earls of Crawford, Montrose and Erroll came up against Surrey, Lord Dacre and Thomas Howard – Lord High Admiral and Surrey's other son - who all thus bore the brunt of the battle while the Scots right, commanded by the Earls of Argyll and Lennox maintained their position but, distracted by the rest of the action, were attacked and swiftly dispersed by Sir Edward Stanley on the English left flank!

At this point another huge problem arose, particularly in the bloody melee at the centre of the battle, in that most of the Scots infantry were equipped with long pike's which had proved very effective on the continent, but were useless on this type of terrain which was nothing short of a morass. This made them vulnerable to the English soldiers who were equipped with the much shorter billhook and this is where, and why, the Scots suffered most of their horrific casualties including the death of King James himself! After his surprise attack on, and defeat of the Scottish right, Stanley turned his attention to the bloodbath in the centre, outflanking the main Scottish force and effectively administering the coup-de-grace to the proceedings, the Scots were routed!

The Aftermath

Lord Home was never to be forgiven for his "desertion", the subsequent death of the King and the consequential rout of the largest Scottish army ever assembled! When pressed to go to the King's aid he reportedly commented "we have done our bit, let others do as well"! His actions, or lack of them, were rewarded by his eventual execution for treason by the Governor John Stewart, 2nd incumbent of the 2nd creation of the Duke of Albany, three years later in 1516! A particularly unsavoury incident occurred immediately after the battle in that a force of about five hundred French mercenaries who had fought with the Scots were set upon and slaughtered to a man by the retreating, or

143

fleeing, Scots soldiery! The English now also set about the non-combatant parts of the Scots invasion force that were caught, undefended, on the wrong side of the border and one can only imagine the indiscriminate slaughter and atrocities which were perpetrated there!

In the days that followed, the guns captured by Surrey were taken to Etal Castle for safe-keeping whilst the bodies of the Scots nobility, and there were plenty of them, were retrieved from the battlefield and eventually repatriated, probably by the Nuns of Coldstream Priory! In Edinburgh, panic had set in with the expectation that Surrey would continue north to claim the City and construction was immediately started on the "Flodden Wall" to defend it; whereas in actual fact the thrifty Earl had dismissed the vast majority of his army within a week of the battle to avoid paying them for any longer than was absolutely necessary so even then, money was the bottom line! Parts of the Flodden Wall can still be seen today in Greyfriars Kirkyard. The aforementioned John Heron (the bastard) and his border Rievers, who had played an important part in the early development of the battle by going to the aid of the hard pressed Howard assailed by Home and Huntley, now blotted his copy book by reverting to type - after all they were Rievers – and indiscriminately plundering both the Scots and the English support camps!

Flodden was the undisputed single, biggest by far, military catastrophe ever suffered by

Scotland in all of its history! The Battle of Flodden, or Flodden Field, or sometimes the Battle of Branxton, or Brainston Moor, was an onslaught between Scotland and England in Northumbria where something like 16,000 men died, eighty to eighty five per cent of them Scots, in just over three hours! The Battle of Flodden threw almost every Scottish Family, from the highest, literary, to the lowest, into bitter grief – so many were the slain – and as a mark of respect at their loss in this fatal battle, we owe the origin of one of the best known of Scots dirge's, the heart-rending pipe lament, "Flowers o' the Forest" with its all-pervasive mood! This then, is the epitaph of King James IV; the sixth continuous Stewart monarch!

Rumours persisted, with little or no foundation, that James had survived the battle and gone into exile, or that his body was buried in Scotland. Two Scottish castles in the borders, Hume and Roxburgh, claim to be the real last resting place of the King. Both of them support legends of a skeleton with a chain round its waist being discovered some years after the battle but in both cases, any evidence which did exist was lost. Another legend has the body, complete with chain, being discovered at Berry Moss near Kelso but again with no proof. All these rumours

145

were probably given substance by another one, and that is that during the battle, four supernatural horsemen swept across the field snatching up the King's body as they went as such a prize could not be allowed to fall into the hands of the English after such a humiliating defeat as this! Not surprisingly, there were no available eye witness's of this spectacular event!

The Reformation of Religion in Scotland

After much deliberation, not a little soul searching and at the possible cost of appearing prejudiced (which I refute), I have decided at this point to include an excellent article (in italics) I came across during my research and which explains, to me anyway, what happened in Britain in the early and middle parts of the sixteenth century as regards religion, which from now on, whether we like it or not, plays a progressively important part in this chronicle of the Stewart Dynasty! I think it also explains how both sides regard each other even today, which tends to range from a grudging acceptance right through to vitriolic vilification!

"From the time of Malcolm Canmore's wife, St. Margaret, and probably before, the people of Scotland, en- bloc, had followed the Catholic Church, led by the Pope in Rome. They went to Mass, prayed to God and the Saints and gave money for holy statuary and family memorials. They also paid the Church to forgive their sins

and guarantee their souls a place in heaven. It was however, very remote from most people as its services were in Latin, which only a handful understood. Mainly because of this, by around 1520, religious reformers known as "Protestants" began to call for new ways of worshipping! They wanted Churches to be plain and simple and devoid of pomp and Idolatry, priests to be likewise, and services to be held in a language that all could understand. They also wanted the Bible to be translated from Latin so that ordinary people could read it!"

Now this, as far as it goes, does not strike me as being unreasonable, I think it represents a perfectly fair and valid point of view which was obviously shared by a lot of people at the time! So what happened? Basically, I think it is a question of the break-away Protestants, instead of being happy in establishing their own Church, now sought to deny the Catholics the very same freedom of choice which they themselves had sought; having broken away, they now wished to destroy the "evil" Church of Rome and all it stood for! The Catholics, for their part, obviously felt severely threatened by what they tended to see as this heretical spawn of Satan riding roughshod over everything they revered and held dear! And so it began, ignorance and fear bred intolerance and bigotry on both sides of the divide and the die was cast for generations to come, indeed, ad-infinitum! The article continues:-

"In Scotland, these calls were led by George Wishart and John Knox both of whom the Catholic Queen Mother, Mary of Guise saw as a threat. Wishart was burnt as a heretic in 1546 and Knox was exiled in 1547 but this did not stop him writing or preaching. In 1558 he published "The First Blast of the Trumpet against the Monstrous Regimen of Women", a book strongly criticizing female rulers such as Mary of Guise and her daughter, Mary Queen of Scots. In 1560 Knox was responsible for encouraging the "Reformation Parliament" to ban the Catholic faith forthwith and replace it with a new, Protestant one, to be run on Presbyterian lines with no bishops, priests or monks, these being replaced with elders and deacons, to be chosen by the congregation!"

The people and events mentioned here, in this brief aside, are gone into in more detail in the following chapters and which I hope will lend clarification to what was an emerging problem then and is still a big problem today in many parts of the country!

James Stewart, King James V, 1513 – 1542

Born on the 10th of April 1512 and crowned King of a devastated Scotland on the 21st of September, twelve days after his father's death at Flodden, this was another young man who had a mountain to climb from the start! He was christened at Linlithgow Palace on the 11th of April 1512 and duly received the titles of Duke of Rothesay as well as Prince and Great Steward of Scotland. He reigned until his death on the 14th of December 1542 which followed another heavy Scottish defeat at the Battle of Solway Moss. His only surviving legitimate child, Mary, whose two elder brothers both died in infancy, succeeded him to the throne when she was just six days old! The Scots were reluctant to accept James's English mother, Margaret Tudor, as a regent for the young King and after her remarriage – in secret - on the 8th of August 1514 to Archibald Douglas, the 6th Earl of Angus, they replaced her with James IV's cousin, the Duke of Albany who was to subsequently order the execution of Lord

Home in 1516 for his part in the disaster at Flodden!

Queen Margaret's tempestuous private life had played havoc with her son's childhood and in the autumn of 1524 she dismissed his regents and he was declared an adult ruler by his mother! This meant the end of the line for the Duke of Albany and Robert, 5th Lord Maxwell, another member of the Council of Regency, among others. The young King's mother and stepfather were separated in 1526 and finally divorced in March 1527. Before that though, his stepfather had virtually kidnapped young James in 1526 and for two years held him captive while showering him with gifts and introducing him to many, mostly unsuitable, pleasures. James loathed the man and finally escaped from his clutches in 1528 when he assumed the reins of government himself. James's personal rule began by savagely pursuing his opponents and he proceeded to hound his stepfather, the Earl of Angus out of the country, forcing his family into exile and besieging their castle of Tantallon. He then turned his attentions to the border rebels and the chiefs of the Western Isles.

He combined his suspicions of the nobles around this time with a popular touch, by travelling alone and anonymously among his people as the

"Guidman o' Ballengeich"! On one such sojourn, so the story goes, he was set upon by five gypsies at Cramond Brig, just outside Edinburgh. Heavily outnumbered, he was getting the worst of the deal when a farm labourer, hearing the melee, ran to his aid and between the two of them, they saw of the gypsies. The King then asked his Good Samaritan who he was and the man replied "Jock Howison, a labourer at nearby Braehead farm" then Jock asked the King who he was. James replied that he was a servant at the Royal Court and asked him if he would like to see the King, "aye, I would" replied Jock, and they duly made arrangements to meet outside the Palace gates in Edinburgh the following week.

Before entering the Place when they met the next week, James asked Jock what he wanted above anything else in the world and Jock replied that he would like to own the farm he worked on. Jock then asked James how he would know the King when he saw him as he had never set eyes upon the man before. "Easy" said James, "when the King enters a room everyone else takes their hats off". As they entered a roomful of nobles this indeed happened and James turned to Jock and said "well"?

"Well it must be either you or me" said Jock!

"I am indeed the King" said James, "and you own your farm Jock, thank you"!

There is proof, circumstantial though it may be that James did indeed act out this part of the "Guidman o' Ballengeich", although whether the legend of Cramond Brig is true or not is another matter; regardless of its veracity, I thought the tale well worth the telling! A local character and emergent instigator – destined for fame or infamy depending on your point of view - called John Knox, was said to have described James thus, "He was called by some, a good poor man's King; of others he was termed a murderer of the nobility, and one that had decreed their whole destruction"! Is this an oblique reference to the "Guidman" by Knox? There actually is a statue somewhere in Stirling Castle which is said to depict this character; "Guidman" means landlord or farmer, while "Ballengeich" is a nickname for a road next to the Castle and in Gaelic means "windy pass". James's nickname among the people was "the King of the commons" but among the nobility he was referred to as "the ill-beloved"! All of this points to James V being a bit of a "Jekyll and Hyde" character, and whichever face showed depended entirely upon who he was dealing with at the time.

James increased the royal wealth by tightening control over his estates, and from the profits of justice, customs and feudal rights. He was also not averse to diverting substantial sums of Church monies into his own coffers either! A large amount of this acquired wealth was lavished on building work at Stirling Castle as well as Holyrood, Linlithgow, and Falkland Palaces. Not a few shillings were also invested on tapestries for the decoration of these abodes. James also further increased his income by getting Pope Clement VII to allow him to tax the incomes from the many monasteries in the country. By these moves, it can only be fair to question his much vaunted devotion to Catholicism, which obviously only went so far and counted for only so much! In 1532 James was responsible for the foundation of the Court of Session in the Scottish parliament and which still exists today.

Domestic and international policy were now starting to be affected as a result of James's uncle, Henry VIII of England, having split from Rome and Catholicism and starting the English reformation around 1533. Henry tried to convince James to follow his lead but James was having none of it, he was devout, except in fiscal matters of course, and did not tolerate heresy, as he saw it, so a number of outspoken Protestants were subsequently persecuted. This was nothing new in Scotland however as the persecutions had begun some years previous to this with the burning at the stake of one Patrick Hamilton at St Andrews in 1528!

By 1536 James had decided to marry. The Treaty of Rouen signed on the 26th of August 1517 between France and Scotland, dictated that if the Auld Alliance was to be maintained, then James was obliged to wed a French royal bride. King Francis I of France didn't appear to be too keen on this idea as he insisted that his daughters were either promised elsewhere or were too sickly. After much too-ing and fro-ing, the terms of the Treaty were eventually fulfilled at the Cathedral of Notre-Dame on the 1st of January1537 when James was married to the Princess Madeleine, daughter of the French King. In the event it transpired that Francis had been telling the truth about the health of his daughters as Madeleine died of tuberculosis shortly after arriving in Scotland in July 1537! James, who was a highly strung and intelligent man who suffered from intermittent and melancholic mood swings, was much distressed by this turn of events.

So overwrought was he that within the year, on the 12th of June 1538 to be precise, James married, by proxy, Mary of Guise; daughter of the Duke of Guise and widow of Louis II d'Orleans, Duke of Longueville. Mary already had two sons by her previous marriage and her union with James produced two more, twins, who unfortunately died in infancy within hours of each other in April 1541. Before they died however, they were christened James, Duke of Rothesay and Arthur, Duke of Albany – the third creation of that title – respectively. James and Mary did produce a third child, Mary, who was born on the 8th of December 1542 at Linlithgow Palace and who was destined to become the tragic Mary, Queen of Scots, the King's only legitimate heir! James did have two other recognised sons, James, Earl of Moray born in 1531 and Robert, Earl of Orkney born in 1533, both of whom though were illegitimate and therefore had no claim to the throne.

The death of James's mother on the 18th of October 1541 removed any lingering incentive for peace with England and hostilities inevitably broke out, again! The Scots got the better of the early skirmishes, particularly at the Battle of Haddon Rig on the 24th of August 1542 where the English outnumbered the Scots almost two to one. Led by George Gordon, the 4th Earl of Huntley, the Scots inflicted heavy losses in a significant victory. Unfortunately, this was not a precursor for what was to come. James was at Lauder with his army on the 31st of October and his intentions were to invade England, his nobles though, were reluctant to say the least. He returned personally to Edinburgh, writing a letter to his wife from Falahill on the way, saying that "he had suffered three days of illness". This was possibly the reason that James had failed to attend a meeting at York with Henry who, incensed by this apparent snub, launched a full scale invasion of Scotland.

This culminated in the Battle of Solway Moss on the 24th of November 1542 where the English, outnumbered by five to one this time, more than made up for their defeat at Haddon Rig three months before by handing out a serious and comprehensive hammering; indeed, almost another Flodden! This was due in no small part to Robert, Lord Maxwell and Sir Oliver Sinclair de Pitcairnis being at loggerheads as to who was in overall charge and thus led to a total breakdown in the command structure of the 16,000 or so strong Scottish army. James himself must accept at least a share of the blame for this shambles as, on the one hand he had charged Maxwell with assembling the army but on the other, he had entrusted Sinclair with his royal standard for the conflict as he himself was not going to be able to be present at the battle due to health issues.

James reportedly suffered a complete nervous collapse after this debacle and took to his bed in Falkland Palace with a high fever. When told that his wife had given birth to a daughter instead of the hoped for son, he is credited with saying "it cam wi a lass and it'll gang wi a lass", this being a direct reference to the Bruce's daughter Marjorie, who had brought the crown into the Stewart family with her son, Robert II in 1371. It was also a reference to his daughter Mary, who, he believed, as a woman, would not be strong enough to rule his troubled nation. James V of Scotland died on the 14th of December 1542 and was buried at Holyrood Abbey in Edinburgh!

The Honours of Scotland

It was my original intention to tack this section on to the start of the chapter which now follows this one, the chapter on Mary, Queen of Scots, as she was the first recipient of these Honours at her coronation as an infant in Stirling Castle in 1543. In retrospect however, as I began to see what was involved during my research, I eventually decided against this, slowly forming the opinion that the Honours fully merited a chapter, albeit a brief one, in their own right. The crest on the front cover of this book depicts the red lion of the Kings of Scots with these Honours which are also known collectively as the "Scottish Regalia" and the "Scottish Crown Jewels". They are the oldest set of crown jewels in the British Isles – compliments of Oliver Cromwell – dating as they do from the 15th century although their first use at a coronation wasn't until the 16th. Today they are on permanent display at Edinburgh Castle.

They were used for the coronations of the Scottish monarchs Mary I in 1543 - James VI in

1567 – Charles I in 1633 and Charles II in 1651. Since then they have been used to represent Royal Assent to Legislation in both the Parliament of Scotland – which is the pre Act of Union 1707 parliament – and the Scottish Parliament – which is the post 1997 referendum one – and have also been used at State occasions. These include King George IV's visit in 1822 and the first visit by our own monarch, Queen Elizabeth II, as Sovereign in 1953. After 1707 the Parliament of Great Britain operated for both Scotland and England thus creating the United Kingdom of Great Britain! After 1707 the Honours were considered redundant and were locked away in a chest in Edinburgh Castle until Sir Walter Scott instigated a search for them in 1818. After discovery they were put on public display until 1941 when they were hidden again due to fears of a German invasion. They remained so until 1953 when they were presented to the newly crowned Queen Elizabeth after which they were returned to the Crown Room where they were joined by the Stone of Destiny in 1996!

To backtrack a bit to 1653, when Oliver Cromwell became Lord Protector of England, Scotland and Ireland, he ordered all the English regalia to be broken up and melted down, primarily to obliterate the symbols of monarchy but also, and more importantly, to finance his war-mongering over the years; the Tudor State Crown alone was reputed to be worth a couple of million in today's money! To prevent a similar fate happening to the Scottish Honours, they were spirited away firstly to Dunnottar Castle, which was later besieged by Cromwell's New Model Army, and then to Kinneff Parish Church where they were concealed under the floor until after the Restoration in 1660. Although recovered, they were no longer used to crown Scottish sovereigns.

Today, on occasions such as the opening of the Scottish Parliament, the crown is carried before the Queen by the Duke of Hamilton who is the hereditary bearer of the Crown of Scotland by right of his subsidiary title, Lord Abernethy. Due to their age and condition however, the Sword and the Sceptre are considered to be too delicate to be alongside the Crown on such occasions. To finish, let's have a look at each of the Honours individually –

The Crown, in its present form dates from 1540 when it was remodelled for James V. The original dates from at least 1503 where it is depicted worn by James IV in a portrait painted at his wedding to Margaret Tudor.

The Sceptre, this was a gift from Pope Alexander VI to James IV in 1494. It was remodelled and lengthened in 1536 and is basically made of silver gilt with a finial of polished Cairngorm rock and a Scottish fresh water pearl.

The Sword, also a Papal gift: this time from Pope Julius II to James IV in 1507. An example of Italian craftsmanship, it measures 1.35 metres in length with a silver gilt handle, it was damaged in 1653 as it had to be broken in half to enable it to be properly concealed from Cromwell and his marauding roundheads. Considering the origins of the Sceptre and Sword in particular, what wouldn't Cromwell or John Knox have given to have got their hands on them! And now, after that brief, but I think worthwhile interlude, back to the Stewarts!

Mary Stewart, Queen Mary I, 1542 – 1567

The tragic Mary, Queen of Scots! Born on the 8th of December 1542, her reign began six days later with the death of her father, James V, on the 14th of that month.   Mary was Queen Regnant – monarch in her own right – of Scotland from the 14th of December 1542 to the 24th of July 1567 and Queen Consort – wife of a reigning monarch – of France from the 10th of July 1559 to the 5th of December 1560.   The infant Mary was crowned at Stirling Castle on the 9th of September 1543, which was the very first use of the existing Honours of Scotland and which are also the oldest regalia in the British Isles, bar none! (See previous chapter) Mary's sad life came to an abrupt end twenty years after her abdication, at Fotheringhay Castle Northamptonshire on the 8th of February1587, with her execution which she endured with all the courage and dignity that her lineage and position demanded!

The first regent of Mary's minority rule was the Protestant 2nd Earl of Arran, James Hamilton, who had seen off a challenge from the Catholic Cardinal Beaton, who was already the infant Queen's Chancellor, to become so. Arran, who had originally supported the Treaty of Greenwich, which was basically a marriage contract between Mary and the Prince of Wales, the future King Edward VI, converted to Catholicism in the autumn of 1543 and switched his allegiance to the pro-French faction, consenting to Mary's proposed marriage to the French Dauphin, the future King Francis II, instead! His repudiation of the Treaty and joining of the Catholic revival, instigated by the Earls of Huntley, Lennox and Bothwell, infuriated Henry VIII and led, not surprisingly, to the seven year war with England known as the "rough wooing" which was declared on the 20th of December '43. This wasn't just a political war however; it also had a very strong religious aspect as the Scots were refusing to have Henry's reformation imposed upon them.

This led to much looting and burning in the Scottish borders and lowlands which was eventually brought to a halt, temporarily at least, by a decisive Scottish victory at the Battle of Ancrum Moor on the 17th of February 1545 where the Scots, led by Arran and Archibald Douglas, the 6th Earl of Angus and outnumbered by more than two to one by the English, won the day in great style. The following year, Cardinal Beaton had George Wishart, a Scottish religious reformer and Protestant martyr, burnt at the stake at the castle of St Andrews! Wishart, a mentor to John Knox, had been investigated for heresy in 1538 and again in 1539. Beaton in his turn was shortly after assassinated by Protestant sympathisers – at the suspected instigation of Henry VIII - and his naked and mutilated body hung outside a window of the castle and left to feed the crows! The English King died of ill health caused by his obesity on the 28th of January 1547 and was succeeded by his son, Edward VI.

The Scots, again led by Arran and Angus and this time outnumbering the English by two to one, now took a hammering at the Battle of Pinkie Cleugh on the banks of the river Esk at Musselburgh, on the 10th of September 1547. Immediately after this it was deemed advisable to move the young Queen to a place of safety at Inchmahome Priory near Stirling. Almost a year of unrest and confrontation followed the disaster at Musselburgh, throwing the borders and the south east into upheaval and during which Mary was moved even further west to Dumbarton Castle for her own safekeeping. On the 7th of July 1548 the Treaty of Haddington was signed which betrothed Mary to the French Dauphin, a month later she sailed for France to spend the next thirteen years of her life, and virtually all of her adolescence, at the French Court!

In March 1550 the Treaty of Boulogne was negotiated and peace was declared first of all between France and England and then in June 1551 between Scotland and England. In July 1553 Edward VI died to be replaced by the Catholic Mary Tudor, fondly known as "Bloody Mary" as she reversed her predecessor's Protestant leanings with a Catholic restoration and set about a nationwide persecution by having some 280 religious dissenters burnt at the stake! It should be appreciated at this point, that up until Mary Stewart's ascension to the Scottish throne in 1542, all the troubles between Scotland and England had more or less been on a personal or political level, an ongoing power struggle if you will, between first the Plantagenet's and then the Tudors on the one hand and the Stewarts on the other.

But now, with the conversion of one John Knox to Protestantism in 1543, religion, and its vitriolic consequences, was beginning for the first time to make its presence felt by adding a third dimension to the already volatile mix of the general Scotland – England aggravation, and in a big way at that! Henry VIII had started the ball rolling with his English reformation in 1533 which had little or nothing to do with Theology but was really all about Henry's wishes to marry and divorce on a whim! One can only assume that if something akin to the polygamous "religions" we have today had been around in these days, Henry would simply have converted to one of those and saved himself and Rome an awful lot of trouble, but perhaps I'm being a bit facetious and cynical here!

Arran was created Duke of Chatellerault and made a Knight of the Order of St. Michael in April 1554 for his work in arranging Mary's marriage to the Dauphin. Simultaneously he surrendered the regency to Mary's mother, Mary of Guise who then held the regency until her death due to the onset of dropsy in 1560. In December 1557 the Scottish Earls of Glencairn, Argyll and Morton plus John Erskine of Duns signed the first bond designed to overthrow the Catholic Church in Scotland. Then on the 24th of April 1558, Queen Mary and the Dauphin Francois were married in Notre Dame Cathedral and where also, a secret condition of the marriage contract was signed stating that should Mary die without issue, Scotland would then be gifted in its entirety to France! Later that year, on the 17th of November, Mary Tudor died and Elizabeth I, a cousin of Mary Queen of Scots, was crowned. Elizabeth immediately set about another reformation, reversing her older half sister Mary's re-establishment of Catholicism with another Protestant reign, and so the religious merry – go – round, now in full swing, continued unabated!

On the 10th of July 1559 Mary's husband, the Dauphin, became King Francis II with the death of his father, Henry II, making Mary, Queen Consort of France as well as the Queen Regnant of Scotland! Francois' reign wasn't destined to last very long however, as he picked up an ear infection whilst out hunting in November 1560 and subsequently died on the 5th of the following month. Unproven rumours abounded that he was poisoned but the ear infection spreading into a brain infection seems to be a more likely explanation. Mary immediately lost her French crown to her ambitious mother in law, Catherine of Medici, - the two of them had never seen eye to eye - who became regent for her other son, Charles IX. Mary left Paris for Calais with her entourage on the 25th of July 1561 and sailed from there for Scotland on the 14th of August, arriving in the Port of Leith on the 19th.

Mary's return to Scotland was against all the best advice of her friends as she was now returning to an officially Protestant country after religious reforms led by John Knox who had been very active in her absence. (See the reformation of religion). Amongst other things he had abolished kneeling at communion, had introduced a form of Calvinism and advocated rebellion against "ungodly rulers", sermonised vociferously on "Idolatry" and had been instrumental in the formation of a Reformation Parliament in 1560, adopting a "Protestant Scots Confession" thus breaking with the Pope and the Catholic Church! Knox wrote the "History of the Reformation of Religion in Scotland" six years before his death in 1572. His house can be seen today on the left hand side of Edinburgh's High Street going down towards Holyrood Palace; there is a statue of him in St Giles Cathedral and he is buried beneath what is now parking place No 23 at the rear of that same Cathedral. Hardly a distinguished conclusion to an eminent and vociferous life!

Although a Catholic, Mary was assured on her return to Scotland that she would be allowed to worship as she saw fit and she received an unexpectedly warm welcome from her

Protestant subjects. Around now in 1563, an act was passed by parliament making witchcraft punishable by death! Consequently hundreds of "witches" were tried and put to death, the last one being at Dornoch in 1722.   Initially, Mary ruled with some success and in moderation, advised as she was by her half brother, Lord James Stewart and William Maitland of Lethington who was a subtle politician and diplomat. Since landing at Leith in August '61 Mary had kept a low profile politically and religiously, while travelling the country far and wide both to see and be seen by the people. This approach had worked fine until she stumbled across her nemesis-to-be, the Lord Darnley, at Wemyss Castle on the 16th of February 1565, he promptly followed her back to Edinburgh and where, in the April she nursed him through a bout of measles. It must have been quickly apparent that they were a wee bit more than just friends as Moray, Ruthven, Morton, Glencairn and Chatellerault all signed a bond to try and prevent any possibility of marriage between them.

In the May of '65, Mary made Darnley the Earl of Ross, Lord Robert Stewart the Earl of Orkney and Shetland and Lord Erskine the Earl of Mar. Two months later she issued a proclamation saying she would not interfere in any religious matters and also sought Papal dispensation for her upcoming marriage to Darnley as they were first cousins and blood relatives. She did not however, wait for it to arrive and on the 29th of July 1565, they were married in the chapel at Holyrood Palace. This ill advised marriage however, was simply to initiate an unfortunate and tragic series of events which were to be made even worse by the factious Scottish nobles. These became known as the "chaseabout raids" – so called because the protagonists chased each other around the country without actually coming to blows - which started on the 26th of August with Mary setting out towards Stirling to confront her treacherous half brother, James Stewart, the 1st Earl of Moray (the fifth creation of the title) and his rebellious Lords.

Moray's gripe was over Mary's marriage to Darnley and a subsequent fear of the country sliding back into Catholicism and was later to state that he was only interested in the "maintenance of the true religion". In the October, Mary and Darnley arrived at Lochmaben with their forces to set up camp, attending a banquet in the castle that night. In the meantime Moray fled south to try and elicit help for his campaign from Elizabeth but was severely censured by her for being "a rebel to his Queen" and sent packing. He wintered at Newcastle and returned to Scotland on the 10th of March 1566. While at Lochmaben, Mary met the Earl of Bothwell and made him her Lieutenant General when he joined her campaign. In March '66, the spoiled and petulant Darnley, now temporarily estranged from Mary, signed a bond with the rebel Lords, the objects of which were to uphold the Protestant faith, remove Mary's secretary David Rizzio, and convey the crown matrimonial from Mary to his own person! This effectively meant that were Mary to die, Darnley would become King! Maitland cleverly avoided any part of this, a true politician!

Rizzio was savagely stabbed to death in front of a heavily pregnant Mary at Holyrood Palace on the 9th of March 1566 by one Patrick Ruthven and the Earl of Morton's men with Darnley lurking in the background. Mary was detained at Holyrood while the Lords issued a proclamation in Darnley's name, pardoning the leaders of the chaseabout raids. This all coincided conveniently with the return of Moray from Newcastle who, no doubt with tongue firmly in cheek, expressed his surprise at the murder of Rizzio! With the help of Bothwell and her equerry Arthur Erskine,

Mary and Darnley escaped from Edinburgh to Dunbar castle where she was joined by Huntley, Fleming, Seton, Atholl and Balfour and where she also offered to agree to the pardons of the perpetrators of the chaseabout raids. She refused point blank though, to pardon any of those involved in the murder of Rizzio with the result that Morton, Lindsay and Ruthven fled to England while Maitland fled north and John Knox west to write his "History of the Reformation of Religion in Scotland"!

Later in the month, Mary returned to Edinburgh and accepted Moray, Glencairn and Argyll back into her council, she then retired to the castle there to await the birth of her and Darnley's child in safety. The midwife, Margaret Aestane, was sent for in early June along with the relics of St Margaret and after a long and painful labour; James VI of Scotland was born on the 19th of June 1566. He was to inherit the Scottish throne through his mother's abdication on the 24th of June 1567; and also inherited the English throne as James I through the death of his mother's cousin, Elizabeth I, on the 24th of March 1603 thus making history by becoming the first monarch to rule both Scotland and England simultaneously!

By November 1566 suggestions were being put to Mary that "the Darnley problem" should be solved by his assassination but which she rejected out of hand. On the 17th of December that year, James VI was baptised a Catholic at Stirling Castle Chapel and where the Godparents, in abstentia, were named as the King of France, the Duke of Savoy and Elizabeth I. Darnley was not in attendance at the ceremony! A week later Mary agreed to pardon the Rizzio murderers while Darnley retreated to Glasgow nursing a dose of syphilis. Mary visited him a month later and persuaded him to return with her to Edinburgh where he was put up at the Kirk o' Fields, a house owned by the Hamilton's, for fear of infecting his son James. On the 9th of February 1567 Mary was in attendance at a page's wedding at Holyrood, having previously spent some time with Darnley, when Kirk o' Field was rocked by an explosion. The naked bodies of Darnley and a servant were found apparently smothered, but with no other visible marks on their bodies, in the adjacent garden!

Bothwell, Moray, Morton and Mary herself were among those immediately suspected of complicity. By the end of the month Bothwell was being generally accepted as the perpetrator of what was now being seen as Darnley's premeditated execution. Mathew Stewart, 4th Earl of Lennox and Darnley's father, demanded that Bothwell be tried before the Estates of Parliament to which Mary agreed but a request for a delay by Lennox to gather evidence was denied! Bothwell was thus subsequently acquitted after a seven hour trial on the 12th of April. A week later Bothwell convinced more than two dozen Lords and bishops to sign his "Ainslie Tavern Bond" in which they agreed to support his aim to marry the Queen. On the 22nd of April Mary visited her son at Stirling for the last time and on her way back to Edinburgh on the 24[th,] she was abducted by Bothwell and his men and taken to Dunbar Castle where he allegedly raped her! The two of them retuned to Edinburgh on the 6th of May and on the 15th they were married according to Protestant rites! Bothwell and his first wife, Jean Gordon, sister of Lord Huntley, had conveniently divorced twelve days previously! This ill fated and ill advised union was to bring about Mary's inevitable ruin.

Originally, Mary had believed that many of her nobles had supported her marriage, but things swiftly turned sour between Bothwell – now created Duke of Orkney and consort of the Queen – and his former peers. To say the marriage proved to be deeply unpopular and divisive is an understatement. The Catholics considered the union to be unlawful since they did not recognise either Bothwell's divorce or the validity of the Protestant service and both sides were shocked at Mary marrying the man accused of killing her husband! Their marriage was tempestuous and Mary became despondent. In the event, twenty-odd Scottish peers, known as the "Confederate Lords", rebelled against the Royal pair and raised an army against them, confronting them on Carberry Hill on the 15th of June. There was, however, no battle as the Royalist force dwindled away through desertion during the negotiations and Bothwell was granted safe passage from the field, compliments of Mary!

The Lords escorted Mary to Edinburgh where the people crowded the streets and decried her as being an adulterous murderer, the following day she was transferred as a prisoner to Loch Leven Castle, a stronghold on an island in the middle of a Loch in Fife where in Mid-July she mis-carried twins, Bothwell obviously being the father. On the 24th of July Mary was forced to abdicate in favour of her one year old son, James VI who was crowned at Stirling on the 29th of the month and Mary's half brother, James Stewart, the Earl of Moray was elected as his regent. Bothwell meanwhile was driven into exile and imprisoned in Denmark where he died insane on the 14th of April 1578. He had been imprisoned in the notorious Dragsholm Castle where he existed in the most appalling conditions; he spent the last ten years of his life in a deep "bottle" dungeon chained to a central pillar around which he wore a groove in the floor! This treatment first robbed him of his sanity and after which, death was a welcome release!

Mary escaped from Loch Leven on the 2nd of May 1568 with the aid of George Douglas, the brother of the castle's owner, Sir William Douglas. After managing to raise an army of 6,000 men, she met Moray's forces at the Battle of Langside on the 13th of May where she was comprehensively defeated and after which she fled south via Dundrennan Abbey to Carlisle where she was taken into custody by local officials on the 18th of May. Mary was now obviously expecting assistance from her cousin, Elizabeth I but this was not readily forthcoming as Elizabeth was hedging her bets due to Mary's strong hereditary claim to the English throne through her Tudor lineage from King Henry VII.

The final nineteen years of Mary's life, though far from dull on a personal level, had little or no further bearing on the destiny's of the Royal
183

houses of Scotland and England, suffice to say she spent them being almost continuously moved around England from one prison to another. Luxurious houses and apartments they may have been but they were still prisons at the end of the day. In 1577 Mary made a will, in which she wished her son to marry a Spanish Princess and revert to Catholicism. The English government then passed the "Act of Persuasion" four years later which made it an act of high treason for anyone to reconcile to Catholicism! Thus, even at the end, religion was still the bugbear of Mary's life, the Catholics hadn't liked her because of her apparent tolerance of Protestantism and the Protestants hadn't liked her because she was a Catholic! On top of that there were often times during her turbulent reign when she incurred the displeasure of her Scottish nobles by being more interested, as they thought, in her claim to the English throne than in the business of running the affairs of her Scottish one. Whilst Mary was never charged, or even openly accused, of Darnley's murder, she was never ever totally cleared of at least the suspicion of complicity in it either.

During those nineteen years, Mary was the focus of a long series of mostly minor, Roman Catholic plots against Elizabeth, culminating in the

"Babington Plot" to assassinate the Queen which led to her minister's demanding Mary's execution. "So long as there is life in her" they said, "there is hope, so as they live in hope, we live in fear"! Mary's final move was to Fotheringhay Castle in Northamptonshire on the 25th of September 1586 where she was executed by beheading on the 8th of February 1587. She met her death with fortitude and dignity. Her son, James VI and I, had his mother's body exhumed from Peterborough Cathedral on the 11th of October 1612 and re-interred in Henry VII's vault – her paternal great grandfather - in Westminster Abbey!

James Stewart, King James VI and I, 1567 – 1625

The man who made history! Born in Edinburgh Castle on the 19th of June 1566 to parents Mary Stewart, Queen of Scots and Henry Stewart, Lord Darnley, who were first cousins and also practising Catholics! James received the crown of Scotland on the 29th of July 1567 and reigned in that country from his mother's abdication on the 24th of June 1567 until the 27th of March 1625. He received the crown of England on the 25th of July 1603 and reigned in that country from the 24th of March 1603 until the 27th of March 1625 thus becoming the first ruling monarch of both countries simultaneously. This was due to his direct Stewart dynasty ancestry on both his mother and his father's sides along with Henry VII of England being his paternal 2G grandfather. The fact that the consecutive English monarch's Edward VI, Mary I and Elizabeth I, who were all Henry VIII's children, and who all died without issue, was also a contributory factor enabling this to happen.

James was baptised in a Catholic ceremony at Stirling Castle on the 17th of December 1566 and where Charles IX of France, Elizabeth I of England and the Duke of Savoy, were named as Godparents through representatives. Mary refused to let the Archbishop of St Andrews spit in the child's mouth as was the custom in these days! The sermon at the young King's coronation in July 1567 was preached by John Knox, and in accordance with the religious beliefs of most of the ruling class of Scotland, James was brought up as a member of the Protestant Church or "Kirk". The Privy Council then selected a team of four tutors for James, the leader and most senior of which was George Buchanan who, through a regime of regular beatings, instilled in him a passion for literature and learning. He also sought to mould James into a God-fearing Protestant King who accepted the limitations of monarchy.

The kingdoms of Scotland and England remained separate sovereign states with their own parliaments, judiciary and laws though they were both ruled by James in a state of personal union, as opposed to a Federation which is ruled by a central government. Four different regents - his uncle, James Stewart the 1st Earl of Moray (5th creation of the title) from 1567 to 1570 – his grandfather, Mathew Stewart the 4th Earl of Lennox (2nd creation of the title) from 1570 to 1571 – John Erskine the 1st Earl of Mar (7th creation of the title) from 1571 to 1572 and James Douglas the 4th Earl of Morton from 1572 to 1581 - ruled his Scottish kingdom during his minority which officially ended in 1578 although he didn't gain full control of his government until 1583. His first regent, Moray, was assassinated by James Hamilton of Bothwellhaugh who was a supporter of Mary with a grudge, the next, Lennox, was carried fatally wounded into Stirling Castle after a raid by Mary's supporters and the third, Mar, died following a banquet at Dalkeith Palace given by the fourth, Morton!

Not surprisingly, poison was suspected but Morton went on regardless to be the most effective of James's regents, and he made enemies in the process. He fell from favour when Frenchman Esme Stewart, Sieur d'Aubigny, a first cousin of Darnley and future 5th Earl of Lennox, arrived in Scotland and swiftly established himself as the foremost of James's powerful male "favourites". Morton was executed on the 2nd of June 1581 belatedly charged with complicity in Darnley's murder while Esme Stewart was elevated to the only Dukedom in Scotland with the title, Duke of

Lennox. The fifteen year old King was to remain under the influence of Lennox for another year. Broadly speaking, James's childhood and adolescence were unhappy, abnormal and at times precarious, the treatment meted out to him by his various guardians and tutors varied widely and his education, though thorough, was weighted with strong Presbyterian and Calvinistic political doctrine, thus he became not only the first of the dynasty to rule two countries but was also its first Protestant monarch!

In 1579 a "poor law" had been enacted by parliament which put in place some pretty severe punishments for "vagabonds and idle beggars". This was to control the administration of help to the growing numbers of poor and destitute, a relentless increase due to a rising population and resultant food shortages. Under this legislation, any able-bodied man who refused work could be placed in the stocks and whipped! It is not clear what input, if any, James had in this particular political nutmeg. Unfortunately, and according to various sources, James allegedly had the same sexual orientation problems as his great-great-grandfather, James III. In August 1582 the Protestant Earls of Gowrie and Angus saw fit to detain the King and chase the Duke of Lennox back to France for apparently pretty blatant displays of "carnal lust"! David Hume, a historian of the Douglas family, is quoted as saying that "while the King was possessed of many virtues, none of them were pure and free from the contagion of neighbouring vices".

Another source describes him as highly intelligent and sensitive but also shallow, vain and exhibitionist who "sought solace with unsavoury and extravagant male favourites". Henry IV of France meantime, labelled him "the wisest fool in Christendom"! On this tack, James was no stranger to religious controversy either, pushing through as he did, the "Black Acts" of 1583 which was legislation to halt the advancement of strict Presbyterianism and Calvinism. Although a Protestant, James was a firm believer in the "Divine Rights of Kings" and in the rights of his bishops to run the Scottish Church. His response to the extremists was "No Bishops, No King"! Overall, James's attempts to curb the power of his nobles and the church were fairly successful. In 1586 James signed the Treaty of Berwick with England which was basically a pact between the two now largely Protestant countries to assist each other in the event of either being attacked by the Catholic countries of France and Spain.

Many saw this as a feint by Elizabeth to soften her next political move, the execution of her first cousin and James's mother, Mary, Queen of Scots, in 1587 and which James apparently denounced as "A strange and preposterous procedure", a typical atypical political statement, making little or no sense to anyone but the maker of it, and even that is probably questionable! He definitely had his eye firmly on the dual monarchy by this time as, during the Spanish Armada crises of 1588, he assured Elizabeth of his support as "your natural son and compatriot of your country". Strictly speaking, he was after all Elizabeth's Godson and the "compatriot" bit probably referred to the Treaty of Berwick.

Throughout his youth James had been praised for his chastity, showing little interest in the opposite sex and after the banishment of Lennox, he continued to prefer male company. A suitable marriage however, had to be arranged to reinforce his monarchy and the fourteen year old Anne of Denmark, younger daughter of the Protestant Frederick II, drew the short straw. Anne sailed for Scotland shortly after a proxy marriage in Copenhagen in August 1589 but was forced into Norway by storms. When James heard of this, he undertook what many called "the one romantic episode of his life", and sailed from Leith with a retinue of many hundreds to fetch his bride to be personally. The couple were formally married at the Bishop's Palace in Oslo on the 23rd of November '89 and returned to Scotland on the 1st of May 1590. James was seemingly infatuated with Anne during their early matrimonial years and showed her much patience and affection. They had seven children, only three of whom survived into adulthood, Henry Frederick, Prince of Wales, who died of typhoid at eighteen, Elizabeth, who became the Queen of Bohemia and grandmother of George I of the House of Hanover who inherited the British throne after the demise of Queen Anne, the last Stewart monarch, and finally Charles, his eventual successor. Anne of Denmark died in March 1619.

James also displayed an interest in the occult in general and witchcraft in particular, a subject which he considered to be a branch of theology. This was probably triggered by his visit to Denmark, a country familiar with witch-hunts, and after his return he visited the North Berwick witch trials, the first major persecution of witches in Scotland under the 1563 Witchcraft Act. James apparently personally supervised the torture of women accused of being witches, most noticeably, one Agnes Sampson, who stood accused of sending storms against James's ships, inspired by this personal involvement, James penned the tract "Daemonologie" in 1597 and which provided the background material for Shakespeare's "tragedy of Macbeth". Also penned by him over '97 and '98 were "The True Law of Free Monarchies" and "Basilikon Doron" (Royal Gift) in which he argued a theological basis for monarchy and was written as a book of instruction for the four year old Prince Harry. In "True Law" he set out the divine right of Kings and proposed an absolutist theory of monarchy seeing Royalty as superior, almost God-like beings! He also commissioned and sponsored "The Authorised King James Version" of the Bible, published in 1611.

Being himself of a scholarly bent, James could probably identify when he was asked to intervene after a riot at the Edinburgh Royal High School on the 15th of September 1595 left a bailiff dead! Apparently, discipline under a Mr Hercules Rollock, then head teacher, had collapsed and the boys had barricaded themselves in, fortifying themselves with ample food and drink. After a day or so it was decided that the boys had to be dislodged and so their barricade was stormed with the resultant death of the unfortunate bailiff, shot by a student called William Sinclair. The riot collapsed with this and the ringleaders spent the next two months in the Edinburgh Tollbooth along with the common riff-raff! Due to their elevated status as children of gentlemen, the boys then claimed they could not be treated impartially by the magistrates and so asked the King to intervene by granting them an assize of Peers of the Realm! James complied and the boys, including Sinclair, walked free! This goes to prove that school shootings are not strictly a modern day malaise!

Accession of the Stewarts in England, Union of the Crowns 1603

Elizabeth I of England was the last of Henry VIII's descendants and James VI of Scotland was seen as the heir to the English throne through his great-grandmother, Margaret Tudor, who was Henry's elder sister. From 1601 certain English politicians, notably Sir Robert Cecil, the future Earl of Salisbury, had maintained a secret correspondence with James in anticipation of a smooth succession upon Elizabeth's impending death. This came about in the early hours of the 24th of March 1603 and James was proclaimed King of England and Ireland in London later the same day! James would have liked his two

Kingdoms to be completely united but each retained their own parliament, church, legal and educational systems; being united only in their crowned heads.

On the 5th of April James left Edinburgh for London promising to return every three years, a promise he reneged upon, returning only once in 1617. He progressed slowly southwards and steadily grew amazed at the wealth of his new land and subjects, he was quoted as saying he was "swopping a stony couch for a deep feather bed". Arriving in the capital on the 7th of May, after Elizabeth's funeral, his new subjects flocked to see him, relieved no doubt that his succession had triggered neither unrest nor invasion! Mobbed by crowds of spectators he was informed that his subjects only wanted to see his face, to which he reputedly replied "God's wounds, I will pull down my breeches and they shall see my arse"! His English coronation took place on the 25th of July with all the pomp and circumstance that that occasion demanded but his English courtiers were wary of their Scottish counterparts, among whom they perceived "favourites" of the King – a reference to his dubious sexuality – and were also distrustful of his "uncouth ways"!

James reigned in all three Kingdoms for 22 years, a period known as the Jacobean era after him, until his death in 1625 at the age of 58. He styled himself "King of Great Britain and Ireland" and during his reign, the Plantation of Ulster and the colonisation of the Americas began. At almost 58 years, his Scottish reign was longer than any of his predecessors, achieving most of his aims in that country in the process. However, the Kingdom to which he now succeeded though was not without its problems. Monopolies and taxation had created widespread grievances and the costs of the "nine years war" – raging since 1594 – had created a heavy burden on the English government. At the time of James's succession, England had incurred debts in the region of £400,000! In today's money this would probably be around many billions!

The "nine years war" ended exactly one week after Elizabeth's death and James's succession and had been a long, expensive and very bitter conflict between England on the one side against Ireland and Spain with Scottish mercenaries thrown in, on the other. Casualties on the English side were in the region of 30,000 though most of these died from disease; on the Irish side, this figure was in excess of 100,000 which included civilians, and the vast majority of these died from famine and disease!   The war was caused by the Irish Chieftains Hugh O'Neill, 2nd Earl of Tyrone, and Hugh Roe O'Donnell, King of Donegal, trying to halt the advance of the English state in Ireland from a relatively small area around what is now Dublin, and called "The Pale" to ruling the entire island. The war was fought in all parts of the country but mainly in the northern province of Ulster and ended in defeat for the Irish chieftains which led to the "Flight of the Earls" and to "The Plantation of Ulster". (This literally meant a re-planting but with humans, not trees)!

"The Flight of the Earls" took place on the 14th of September 1607 when O'Neill, O'Donnell and about ninety followers left Ireland for mainland Europe. This was the end result of the defeat at the Battle of Kinsale in 1601 and the subsequent downturn of their fortunes and eventual defeat in the final two years of the war, followed by a further four years of victimisation by the victorious English government. "The Plantation of Ulster" was, not to put too fine a point on it, a re-colonisation programme of Ulster, a Gaelic speaking Catholic province of Ireland, by English speaking Protestants, mainly Presbyterian Scots. Starting as it did in 1606, King James VI & I saw this as a "civilising" process which he decided, in his wisdom, to make official in 1609.

The England-Irish war and its aftermath apart, James did not have his troubles to seek. His somewhat intolerant religious policy consisted of asserting the supreme authority and divine right of the crown by suppressing both Puritans (right-wing Protestants) and Catholics who objected! Needless to say, this incited some pretty fierce opposition which materialised in the form of the "Main Plot" of July 1603 and an offshoot called the "Bye Plot" which was a conspiracy of Roman Catholic Priests and Puritans who wanted nothing more than religious tolerance for their respective denominations. The Main Plot however was a bit more sinister and was aimed at solving the problems by replacing the King with his cousin Arabella Stewart! These conspiracies led to the arrests of Henry Brooke, Lord Cobham who was the suspected leader, and Sir Walter Raleigh, suspected of financing the plot via Spain, among quite a few others. Both men were sent to the Tower of London for their efforts, Cobham, who was sick, was released the same year but died shortly afterwards. Raleigh was released in 1616 but was executed in 1618 to appease the Spanish after ransacking one of their outposts in South America around late '16 or early '17.

Those of the English nobility who were looking for change were disappointed when James maintained Elizabeth's Privy Councillors in office, as was previously, and secretly, arranged with the shrewd Robert Cecil who was tightly managing things behind the scenes aided and abetted by the Lord Chancellor and Baron Ellesmere, Thomas Egerton; and the Lord Treasurer and Earl of Dorset, Thomas Sackville. The King however, quickly expanded the Privy Council with the addition of five Scottish nobles as well as long term supporters Henry Howard, 1st Earl of Northampton and his nephew Thomas Howard, 2nd Earl of Arundel. These changes left James free to pursue his long-term ambition and dream – a closer union between England and Scotland! In October 1604 James assumed the title "King of Great Britain" by proclamation, as against by statute, and Sir Francis Bacon assured him that he could not use it in any legal proceedings. The commons had already denied him the use of this title on legal grounds. Also in 1604 James had proposed a union between his Scottish and English parliaments but neither appeared keen and the proposal was abandoned.

On the night of the 4th of November 1605, the eve of the state opening of the second session of James's first English Parliament, a man called Guy Fawkes was discovered in the cellars of the parliament buildings. He was guarding a pile of wood close to three dozen barrels of gunpowder with which it was intended to blow up the building the following day while the Parliament was actually in session and therefore causing maximum death and destruction. Fawkes was involved with a small group of English Catholics led by Robert Catesby whose plan was to assassinate the Protestant King and replace him with his daughter, the Princess Elizabeth of Bohemia, as both his sons were to have died with their father in the resultant explosion. The plot had been revealed in an anonymous letter sent to William Parker, 4th Baron Monteagle on the 26th of October and the resultant searches turned up Fawkes and the gunpowder. Any perpetrators who were not killed in outright flight were hung, drawn and quartered to a man!

As James's reign progressed so did his mounting financial pressures, this was due in part to creeping inflation but also to the financial incompetence and profligacy of his own court. In February 1610, Robert Cecil, now elevated to the Earl of Salisbury since 1605, proposed the "Great

Contract", a scheme whereby parliament, in return for ten royal concessions, would grant the King a lump sum of £600,000 to pay off his debts plus an annual grant of £200,000! The ensuing negotiations became so prickly and protracted that James eventually lost all patience and dismissed parliament on the 31st of December 1610. The same pattern was repeated with the "Addled Parliament" of 1614 which James dissolved after a mere nine weeks. James then proceeded to rule without a parliament at all until 1621, using as a stop-gap the employment of officials such as Lionel Cranfield who were adept at the art of assimilating funds for the crown; selling earldoms and other dignitaries specifically created for the purpose as a source of income! Cranfield himself was elevated to the peerage in 1621 and made 1st Earl of Middlesex in 1622!

During this period James lost his Secretary of State, Salisbury on the 24th of May 1612, followed by his eldest son and heir Henry Frederick to typhoid fever on the 6th of November the same year making his younger brother Charles the new heir to the throne. Yet another instance of a Stewart King that would never had been if an older sibling had lived. Henry Frederick had been named after his grandfathers, Henry Stewart Lord Darnley, and King Frederick II of Denmark. James also lost his wife Anne of Denmark on the 2nd of March 1619. The prospect of a dowry from a marriage between his heir Charles and the Infanta (Princess) Maria Anna of Spain were seen as another potential source of income by James, as well as a way of maintaining peace and avoiding the additional costs of a war.

James's problems were further exacerbated by the outbreak of the Thirty Years War in 1618; an extended conflict fought in central Europe and involving most European countries as well as the Holy Roman Empire and was basically, a Protestant versus Catholic confrontation. Matters came to a head when he finally called a parliament 1621 to fund a military expedition in support of his Protestant son-in-law, Frederick V Elector Palatine, who had been ousted from Bohemia by the Catholic Emperor Ferdinand II in 1620. The Commons, on the one hand, granted subsidies which were deliberately inadequate to finance serious military operations in aid of Frederick, and on the other called for war against Spain, no doubt remembering the bonanza days of the Armada! Simultaneously with this, in November 1621, they also called for Prince Charles to marry a Protestant and for the enforcement of the anti-Catholic laws. James warned them in no uncertain manner that they risked the royal wrath if they dared to interfere in the royal prerogative! This provoked them into issuing a statement protesting their rights, including the freedom of speech. The King's answer to that however, urged on by his "special friend" George Villiers, now elevated to Duke of Buckingham, and the Spanish Ambassador Gondomar, was to rip the protest out of the record book and dissolve parliament, yet again!

After his one and only visit to Scotland in 1617, James attempted to force through his "Five Articles of Perth" at the General Assembly of the Church of Scotland in 1618. These were measures intended to bring the worship and government of the Presbyterian Church of Scotland into line with the Episcopalian Church of England and was met with strong opposition. The measures were – kneeling during communion – private baptism – private communion for the sick or infirm – confirmation by a Bishop and observance of the Holy Days of Christmas and Easter! These articles were reluctantly accepted by the General Assembly in 1618, ratified by the Scottish Parliament in 1621 then repealed by the "Confession of Faith Ratification" act of 1690. James, realising his mistake did not try to enforce the Articles and never again tried to introduce ecclesiastical innovations but still left the Church in Scotland divided at his death. Another inherent problem for his son Charles!

And talking of which, this young man, now 22, unilaterally decided to give the Kingdom a taste of what they could expect when he acceded to the throne. In early 1623, he and the Duke of Buckingham, now Charles's own confidante, took it into their heads to court disaster by travelling incognito to Spain to win the Infanta directly. This proved to be a spectacular mistake! The Infanta abhorred Charles and the Spanish confronted them with terms that included the repeal of anti-Catholic legislation by parliament. Although a treaty was signed, the Prince and the Duke returned to England in October without the Infanta and promptly renounced it, much to everyone's delight. Disillusioned and somewhat affronted by their Spanish (in) experience, Charles and Buckingham now turned James's Spanish policy on its head by calling for a French match for the Prince, as opposed to the failed Spanish one, and a war against the Spanish Habsburg Empire for good measure.

James was prevailed upon to call another parliament which met in February 1624 and for once, the outpouring of anti-Catholic sentiment in the Commons was echoed in court, where control of policy was shifting from King James to Prince Charles and Buckingham. They pressurised the King to declare war and engineered the impeachment of the Lord Treasurer, Cranfield, when he opposed the plan on grounds of cost. The outcome of the parliament was unambiguous; James still refused to declare war, but Charles believed the Commons had committed themselves to finance a war against Spain. This stance was to contribute greatly to his problems with parliament in his own reign which was shortly to begin. Charles got his French match when he eventually married Henrietta Maria, the youngest daughter of the French King Henry IV, on the 13th of June 1625, shortly after his accession. This was the first ever arranged marriage between a Protestant Prince and a Catholic Princess in Britain, if not in Europe!

After about the age of fifty and in his declining years, James suffered increasingly from gout, arthritis and kidney stones; he also lost most of his teeth and drank progressively heavily. During the last year of his life, with Buckingham consolidating his control of Charles to ensure his own future, James was often seriously ill and therefore vulnerable to, and powerless over, the personal manipulations and political machinations which were going on around him. He is suspected of suffering from Porphyria, a disease which his descendant George III exhibited symptoms of, as his urine was described as being the "dark red colour of Alicante wine"; this though, could also have been down to the kidney stones. In early 1625 he was plagued by severe arthritis, gout and fainting fits and in the March fell seriously ill with tertian ague, a form of malaria which recurs every second day, and finally suffered a stroke. James died at Theobalds House on the 27th of March after a violent attack of dysentery and with the ever cynical Buckingham at his bedside. His funeral took place on the 7th of May with Bishop John Williams of Lincoln officiating. He was buried in Westminster Abbey though exactly where, was a mystery for many centuries until, after some excavation work, it was found in the vault of Henry VII, beside his mother, Mary!

For all his flaws, James was widely mourned and had largely retained the affection of the people as they had enjoyed uninterrupted peace and relatively low taxation during his "Jacobean Reign". His reputation though, suffered greatly at the hands of some acidic, anti-Stewart historians in the mid-seventeenth century who blamed his tendency for political absolutism, financial irresponsibility and his cultivation of unpopular favourites as laying the foundations for the English Civil War. It cannot be denied either, that he bequeathed his son with a fatal belief in the divine right of Kings and a disdain for parliament which culminated in his execution and the abolition of the monarchy. Under James, the "Plantation of Ulster" had begun as had the colonisation of North America with the foundation of Jamestown Virginia in 1607, followed by Cupar's Cove Newfoundland in 1610 and the landing of the Pilgrim Father's from the Mayflower in 1620.

Throughout his life James had indisputably close relationships with male courtiers and the aristocracy, Dukes and Earls among them, which has been the subject of much debate and conjecture over the centuries. He stands accused of homosexual relations with certain "favourites" on the one hand, while on the other, his wife Anne had a dozen pregnancies, giving birth to seven live children in the process! The Stewarts in general, were subject over the centuries to speculation, misplaced or otherwise, about their sexual orientation, both male and female! In some cases this was mere whispers, in other cases some improprieties were covertly suspected, but in the cases of James III and his great – great – grandson James the VI & I in particular, there are some pretty indisputable grounds for misinterpretation, shall we say, of their questionable behaviour, sexual or otherwise. Personally, I am certainly not going to demonstrate the effrontery to sit in judgement for whatever reason, and it is not the purpose of this book to cast slanderous or libellous allegations upon anybody, particularly as nothing can now be substantially proved or disproved so, as the saying goes today, and as far as I am concerned, the jury is out on this one! I leave it entirely up to the reader to make his or her own mind up about this aspect of the Stewart dynasty!

Charles Stewart, King Charles I, 1625 – 1649

Charles I, like his father, was monarch of the three Kingdoms from the 27th of March 1625; his relentless, unforgiving and continual disputes with both his English and Scottish parliaments though, mostly caused by his inherent egotistical and dogmatic attitude, eventually led to hostilities between England and Scotland, then civil war and finally, to his own execution on the 30th of January 1649! A tumultuous sovereignty indeed, by this the tenth monarch of the dynasty and the second Protestant one, albeit of the Episcopalian, or High Anglican variety which was viewed by many to be Catholicism in all but name! His marriage to the Catholic French Princess Henrietta Maria on the 13th of June 1625 did little to put the country's minds at rest about his religious leanings either; indeed to the contrary, it caused much concern on that front. His new bride's unwillingness to have any part in the Protestant ceremony of his English coronation on the 2nd of February 1626 exacerbated the situation even further but Charles seemed to care little for his personal popularity, and appeared to be contemptuous of other people's opinions, whether valid or otherwise and this was to become a source of much controversy throughout his troubled reign.

To deal with his early life first, Charles was born in Dunfermline Palace, Fife, on the 19th of November 1600 and baptised at a Protestant ceremony in the Royal Chapel of Holyrood Palace, Edinburgh, on the 3rd of December and where he was also created Duke of Albany (fifth creation), the traditional title of the second son of the King of Scotland. He was a weak and sickly infant so when his parents and older siblings, Henry and Elizabeth, left for London in April 1603, Charles was left behind under the guardianship of his father's friend, lord Fyvie. By 1604, at three and a half, he was deemed fit enough to travel south and be reunited with his family. Here he was placed under the charge of Lady Carey who compelled him to wear boots of Spanish leather and brass to strengthen his weak ankles. As well as his physical development, the child's speech development was also slow and he had a stammer for the rest of his life, this was offset however by his self-righteousness egotism and his overly high concept of royal authority.

Charles was created Duke of York (fourth creation) in January 1605 as was customary in the case of the English sovereign's second son and made a Knight of the Bath; Thomas Murray, a Scots Presbyterian, was appointed as his tutor. He eventually conquered his physical infirmities which were probably caused by rickets and became an adept horseman and marksman, even to the extent of taking up fencing! He hero-worshiped his older, taller and stronger brother Henry, Prince of Wales, whom he attempted to emulate at every opportunity, unfortunately though, in November 1612, Henry died of typhoid fever making Charles the heir apparent to his father's Kingdoms of Scotland, England and Ireland and he was subsequently created Prince of Wales and Earl of Chester in 1616. Previously, in 1613, his elder sister Elizabeth had married Frederick V, Elector Palatine of Bohemia, and moved to Heidelberg; this union was to lead directly to the Hanoverian King George I inheriting the British throne in 1714 as the Protestant great - grandson of James VI & I.

After the total failure of Charles's and Buckingham's sojourn to Spain and its aftermath in 1622 / 23 to woo over the Infanta as a bride for the Prince, they duly turned their attention to France and the Catholic Princess Henrietta

Maria, who was to become his eventual bride. Many parliamentarians were against this match on religious grounds but Charles gave them an undertaking that he would not lift restrictions on Catholic recusants and thereby undermine the official establishment of the reformed Church of England! However, in a secret wedding pact with Louis XIII of France, he promised to do exactly that! Worse, he placed under French command an English naval force that would be used to suppress the Protestant Huguenots at La Rochelle!

He further nurtured the general distrust of his religious policies with his support of Richard Montagu, a controversial anti – Calvinist ecclesiastic who was in permanent disrepute among the Puritans. This all added up to Charles being suspected of clandestine attempts to aid the resurgence of Catholicism. By 1624 King James was growing ever weaker and feebler of mind and body and as a result was finding it difficult to control parliament. By his death in March 1625, Charles and his confidante Buckingham had already assumed *de facto* control of the Kingdom. Later that year, a badly run and organised naval expedition against Spain, under Buckingham's leadership, prompted parliament to begin proceedings for impeachment against the Duke. Faced with the prospect of dismissing his friend, Charles opted for dismissing parliament instead!

In the meantime, problems of domesticity were arising and souring the early years of the royal marriage and culminated in the King expelling the vast majority of Henrietta's entourage in August 1626. Shortly afterwards, and despite his earlier agreement to provide ships as a condition of his marriage, Charles now launched an attack on the French coast to defend La Rochelle! This action in 1627, again led by Buckingham, and again a total shambles, led to calls for the Duke's head on a plate; the man was now detested by all bar Charles. On the 23rd of August 1628, Buckingham was assassinated! Charles was bereft and spent the next two days in deep lamentation locked in his rooms! Everyone else was overjoyed! This however, accentuated the gulf not only between Charles's court and the nation, but also the gulf between the crown and parliament as well. The Duke's death, he was ignominiously and fatally stabbed in a Portsmouth pub, effectively ended the Spanish hostilities but not so the ones between Charles and parliament; it did though, lead to an improvement in Charles's married life, Henrietta becoming pregnant for the first time! See the last paragraph of the previous chapter and read into that what you will!

Unfortunately, personal tragedy was to strike and the couple lost that baby, a son, the same day as he was born. He was named Charles James, Duke of Rothesay and Cornwall and was buried as "Charles, Prince of Wales" on the 13th of May 1629. Shortly before this Charles had dismissed his fourth parliament in the March of 1629 and had decided instead to make do without either its advice or the taxes it alone could grant legally. Simultaneously, there came a crackdown on the Puritans and Catholics with the result that many of them migrated to the American Colonies. From March '29 until April '40 Charles ruled without a parliament and this period became known as the "eleven year tyranny"! He was technically within his rights to do this as there was a precedent for it and he raised most of what he needed through imposition and exploitation, making himself extremely unpopular indeed with parliament and the people alike. Among his leading advisors during this period were the most reverend William Laud, Archbishop of Canterbury and Sir Thomas Wentworth, 1st Earl of Strafford (first creation), both efficient and both, like their master, heartily disliked! These fiscal hard times did however have a silver lining; Charles was compelled to bring to an end the wars, mostly of Buckingham's making, with Spain and France.

In the meantime, the royal couple were still improving their relationship and increasing their family as well. After the heartbreak of their first child, Henrietta gave birth a year later, on the 29th of May 1630 to another son, also Charles, who became Charles II and his father's heir. After him came Mary, Princess Royal, on the 4th of November 1631 and who was destined to marry William II, Prince of Orange in 1641. Next came another son, James, on the 14th of October 1633 and he was destined to become James VII & II as his elder brother, Charles II died without issue. After him came three daughters, Elizabeth in 1635, Anne in 1637 and Catherine in 1639; these unfortunately all died young and without issue. Their penultimate child was again a son, Henry, Duke of Gloucester on the 8th of July 1640 and who died aged twenty, without issue. Their last child came four years later on the 16th of June 1644, a daughter called Princess Henrietta Anne who was to marry the Duke of Orleans in 1661. King Charles I was unique so far in the history of the Stewart dynasty, siring two living and crowned Kings as he did, in Charles II and James VII & II! James however, emulated this feat with the births of his two daughters, Mary and Anne, who both became crowned and reigning monarchs in their own right!

Religion, and the open warfare which was to result from it, was now about to show its ugly face again, and with a vengeance! Scotland proved to be the catalyst for this as James VI had, in effect, planted several time bombs when he had re-introduced Episcopacy to the Church of Scotland in 1583 with his "Black Acts "legislation of that year and then increasing the number of bishops after he acceded to the English throne twenty years later! On top of all that, his 1618 introduction of the "Articles of Perth", more anti-Presbyterianism legislation, further fuelled the fires of religious intolerance and bigotry which he bequeathed to his son and heir, and who was found to be very much lacking when it came to dealing with them; indeed, Charles's own close-minded arrogance merely exacerbated the problems to a great extent.

Charles had left Scotland aged three and was to return only the once, for his Scottish coronation in the June of 1633! His Protestant English coronation had taken place in February 1626 and had been snubbed by his Catholic wife. He now proceeded to incense everyone north of the border by insisting that his Scottish ceremony be conducted in the Anglican, or High English rite, which virtually all and sundry viewed as Catholic or at the very least, the next best thing to it. This was held in St Giles Cathedral Edinburgh, next door to which work had started the previous year on the building of a permanent home for the Scottish parliament, Parliament House! Charles had also intended this, his first meeting with his Scottish parliament, or his "Coronation Parliament of 1633" as it was known, to be a showcase of royal power but in an effort to force through controversial laws he disregarded parliamentary tradition and lost the support of many of his influential nobles!

After returning south again and causing much interim nastiness with a lot of conflict in both parliaments, he eventually, in 1637, provoked a riot in Edinburgh (from London) which escalated into general unrest, and eventually open warfare, when he attempted to impose a High Church Liturgy and Book of Common Prayer on the country without prior consultation with either the Parliament of Scotland or the Kirk! The public mobilised around a re-affirmation of the National Covenant in 1638 which called for a parliament and a church free from royal interference and when the General Assembly of the Church of Scotland met in the November it condemned out of hand the new prayer book, abolished Episcopalian style Church government by bishops and adopted Presbyterian style government by elders and deacons instead! To say Charles was not pleased by these events is an understatement!

These edicts led directly to the first and second "Bishops' Wars" of 1639 and 1640. The first, precipitated by Charles as he perceived the Scottish unrest as a rebellion against his authority, resulted in him raising a rag-tag poorly trained army, without parliamentary funds or aid, and marching north to Berwick on Tweed. Once there he chose not to engage the Covenanters as he believed himself to be if not outnumbered, then certainly inferior to the more experienced Scots, many of whom were veterans of the "Thirty Years War" on the continent and led by General Alexander Leslie, 1st Earl of Leven. Instead, he negotiated the "Treaty of Berwick" whereby he secured the dissolution of the Covenanter's interim government but only at the cost of both the Parliament of Scotland and the General Assembly of the Church of Scotland being recalled! This officially ended the first war without a shot being fired, even though both sides unofficially saw it only as a temporary truce to prepare for the next round.

After eleven years of personal rule, Charles was forced to recall his English parliament in April 1640, which was known as the "Short Parliament", who, on querying his requests for funds for a war against the Scots, was promptly dissolved again within weeks for their pains! Hostilities meanwhile, resumed up north with the second Bishops' War when the Scots under Leslie and Montrose crossed the Tweed and in a short space of time, occupied not only Northumberland and County Durham, but also Newcastle as well after the Battle of Newburn, this result had the effect of placing a stranglehold on London's coal supply. The Scots had met with only half hearted resistance during this incursion into English territory and the occupation of Newcastle meant Charles had no option but to call a truce. All this culminated in the signing of the "Treaty of Ripon" on the 26th of October 1640 which was a huge setback and a major humiliation for Charles, stipulating as it did that Newcastle was to be left in the hands of the Scots and that both Northumberland and County Durham were to be ceded to them also! Not only that, but they were to be financially compensated to the tune of £850 a day to maintain their armies there!

This resulted in Charles recalling his "Long Parliament" a week later on the 3rd of November and negotiations dragged on well into 1641 before the "Treaty of London" was signed, bringing these conflicts to at least a temporary and fragile suspension of hostilities. The Irish parliament had also been summoned in early 1640 and had voted in a subsidy of £180,000 for Charles along with a promise to raise an army of 9,000 men for him. Whether these actually materialised or not seems to be a matter of no little doubt and some speculation! The calling of the long parliament, which lasted for four years, resulted in the immediate arrests of Laud and Strafford, who had been the King's advisors in better days! The latter was executed six months later and the former in 1645. The King also agreed that parliament could not be dissolved without its own consent and the "Triennial Act" of 1641 was voted in to ensure that no more than three years could elapse between parliaments.

Charles had also temporarily improved his position in Scotland by securing favour there during only his second, and final, visit to that country between August and November 1641. He finally conceded to the official establishment of Presbyterianism, thereby undoing all of his father's previous work in the opposite direction! This was interpreted by many however, as a loss of face and the King's credibility was significantly undermined! It seemed that now, no matter what he did, he could do no right, and this after virtually re-modelling both his parliaments during 1640 and '41! It should be understood at this point that although Charles was the King of Scotland, England and Ireland, all that was in fact united was the crowns, the parliaments and churches etc of these countries were still separate entities and indeed, although the Scottish and English parliaments were considered equal partners, the Irish parliament was still considered to be subordinate to the English one and was to remain so until the recognition of "Grattan's Parliament" in 1784!

Although a fragile and uneasy state of peace now existed between Scotland and England – it was probably more of a "Mexican Standoff" than a peace – Charles's problems were far from being over as his Kingdom of Ireland was now about to join the fray! The population of Ireland at the rebellion in October 1641 fell into one of three main social, political and religious groups. The first being the original "Gaelic, Catholic" Irish, the second were the "Old English / Norman" Irish, who were chiefly Catholic or at least Episcopalian and loyal to the English crown, and the third were the "New English" Irish, who were Scottish and English Protestants mainly of the Presbyterian and Puritan persuasions who were settling the land, with royal blessing, particularly in the north under the terms of the "Plantation of Ulster", and at the expense of the original Gaelic and Catholic Irish! It doesn't take a Nostradamus to see where all this was headed! The final match to ignite the blue touch paper was the fact that underhand moves had been set afoot to ensure that the Irish parliament stayed subordinate to the English one!

When armed conflict finally flared up between the Gaelic Irish and the New English in late October, the Old English, who, as their name suggests, were descended from English and French aristocracy over a few generations, sided with the Gaelic Irish whilst simultaneously professing their loyalty to the crown. The unrest that had been festering since 1609 had finally exploded! During the month of November alarmist propaganda, mostly untrue or at least exaggerated, of atrocities perpetrated by the Catholics on the New English began to circulate in England which strengthened anti-Catholic feeling there and further damaged Charles's authority. When he called for funds to put down the Irish rebellion, the English parliament distrusted his motivations; members of the commons suspecting that forces raised now could later be used against the parliament itself! A situation fast falling into total anarchy was made worse when rumours reached Charles that his wife was about to be impeached for supposedly colluding with the Irish rebels and he decided to take matters into his own hands! Whatever else he was or was not; Charles could never be accused of being a stranger to controversy or of lacking moral fibre!

The King suspected, probably with justification that some members of his English parliament had conspired circumspectly with the invading Scots during the second Bishops' war and were also conspiring with the Irish rebels now. On the 3rd of January Charles demanded that his parliament should give up the five members of the commons and the one Lord whom he suspected of this subterfuge, on the grounds of high treason. When this was refused, Charles entered the House of Commons on the 4th of January 1642 with an armed guard to arrest the men personally! He had been pre-empted in this however, as the men he was after had already flown the coop and he was forced to retire, empty handed and mightily embarrassed. This episode was a political and personal disaster for the King; no sovereign had ever entered the House of Commons before, far less with an armed guard, and the whole thing was seen as a grave breach of parliamentary privilege. In one fell swoop, Charles had totally destroyed any credibility or sympathy he had left!

Finally, on the 22nd of August 1642, the first English civil war began with the raising of Charles's Standard at Nottingham. He had already sent his wife and eldest daughter abroad for their own safety in the February as the Parliamentarians had quickly seized London and its environs. 1642 also saw some English Parliamentary troops, but mainly a Scottish Covenanter army, sent to Ulster to protect the Protestants there as the Irish Confederate Wars were now raging throughout that country and would continue to do so until 1652. In 1644 however, the Scots were withdrawn from Ulster and sent to fight in the English civil war after the signing of the "Solemn League and Covenant" which was an agreement with the English parliament that, in exchange for the Scottish troops, the Church of England would adopt Presbyterianism in their government as opposed to their favoured Episcopalian style! This period of British history, from 1639 through to 1652, came to be known collectively as the "Wars of the Three Kingdoms", as hostilities were now rampant in one country or the other, and sometimes in all three simultaneously, and was basically all about what people chose to do, or didn't choose to do, on a Sunday morning! The King's inherent attitude, which was one of belligerent intolerance, did little to help matters either!

At the start of the hostilities, Charles's Royalist forces controlled roughly the Midlands, Wales, the West Country and Northern England; he chose Oxford as his Capital and made it his headquarters for the duration. The Parliamentarians controlled London, the South East, East Anglia and the English Navy. A Parliamentary General and moderate called Sir William Walter described the pending confrontations as "this war without an enemy"! After a few preliminary skirmishes the opposing forces finally met head on at Edgehill on the 23rd of October '42 and where the fighting ended inconclusively as the daylight faded. Charles regrouped at Oxford and throughout the winter tried several times to negotiate with civil and Parliamentary delegations but to no avail, as peace talks collapsed the following April. And so the war continued indecisively through 1643, the only large-scale set-to that year being at Newbury, Berkshire, on the 20th of September and which also ended in stalemate.

Two major events in 1644 however, saw the pendulum swing decisively in the favour of the Parliamentarians. The first was the transfer of the Scottish Covenanter Army from Ulster to England and the second was the formation by parliament of the "New Model Army"! This force differed from the other military units of the day in several fundamental aspects; firstly it was designed for service anywhere in the British Isles as opposed to being tied to a single area or garrison; secondly its soldiers were full time professionals as opposed to part time militia; and thirdly a professional officer corps to lead it was established by prohibiting these officers from having seats in either the Lords or the Commons thereby encouraging their separation from political or religious interference in the execution of their duties! This New Model Army was disbanded with the restoration of the monarchy in 1660 and the commander of one of its cavalry troops in the early days was one Oliver Cromwell, who was to rise swiftly nonetheless, to General rank!

Despite this, Charles was successful at the battle of Cropredy Bridge in Oxfordshire on the 29th of

June '44 where the Parliamentary army was led by the aforementioned Sir William Walter, but another Royalist army under the command of Prince Rupert of the Rhine, who was Charles's nephew, took a pounding at the Battle of Marston Moor in North Yorkshire a few days later at the hands of a Parliamentary army led by the Earl of Manchester and Lord Fairfax, a general of the New Model Army. These two were complimented by a Scots Covenanter Army led by the Earl of Leven. The King meanwhile, continued his campaign in the south with some success, defeating the Parliamentarians of the Earl of Essex before fighting at Newbury for a second time as the winter set in, but this was again inconclusive. Further attempts to negotiate a settlement during this winter, as with the previous one, were unsuccessful and both sides instead, re-armed and re-organised.

The die was cast now however, and the Royalists suffered a decisive defeat at the Battle of Naseby in Northamptonshire on the 14th of June 1645. The King and his nephew, Prince Rupert saw Their Royalist force of some 7,500 men virtually destroyed by a New Model Army of 14,000 men led by Generals Fairfax and Cromwell! This was followed by a series of defeats for the Royalists and then the Siege of Oxford from which the

King escaped in April 1646 disguised as a servant. He surrendered to the Scottish Presbyterian Army besieging Newark-on-Trent and was taken northward by them to Newcastle upon Tyne where, after nine months of negotiations, he was delivered up to the Parliamentary Commissioners in January 1647, so ending the first English Civil War!

All however, was far from quiet in either Scotland or Ireland! The Scots in particular were still smarting from Charles's earlier unbridled arrogance in his attempts to raise taxes without parliamentary approval and, most of all, at his attempted imposition of a Catholic style prayer book and bishops without prior consultation with the General Assembly of the Church of Scotland! This all led to the birth of the Covenanter movement and the Bishops' Wars of 1639 and '40 as related earlier. After much involvement of Scottish forces in both Ireland and England, a full scale civil war broke out in Scotland in 1644 and 1645 between the Royalist supporters of Charles led by James Graham, 1st Marquis of Montrose and the Covenanters, who had controlled Scotland since 1639 and were allied with the English Parliamentarians. The Covenanters, after some early setbacks were eventually victorious despite the addition of an expedition of Gaelic

Irish troops sent to aid Montrose. This expedition took place in spite of the fact that the Confederate Irish Catholics were not only fighting amongst themselves but also against piecemeal incursions of English parliamentary forces and is probably one of the best examples of the collective insanity of this era!

A divide was now not only forming, but widening, between the English Parliament which was favouring army disbandment and Presbyterianism, and the New Model Army which was independent, non-conformist and seeking a greater political role. Charles was more than eager to exploit this split but, despite various negotiations from various places, finished up as the prisoner of the Parliamentary Governor of the Isle of Wight at his Castle of Carisbrooke. From there, and in direct contrast to his earlier conflicts with the Church of Scotland, he managed to sign a treaty on the 26th of December 1647 with them which was known as "The Engagement", and under which the Scots would undertake to invade England on the King's behalf and restore him to the throne, on the condition that Presbyterianism be established in England for a minimum period of three years afterwards. In May 1648 the Royalists rose, igniting the second English Civil War and the

Scots, as agreed, invaded. Uprisings in Kent, Essex, Cumberland and South Wales were put down by Cromwell and the New Model Army and the Scots were comprehensively defeated by it at the Battle of Preston in August 1648 and with that result, went any remote chance the Royalists were entertaining of winning this, the second English civil war!

With no other recourse left open to him, Charles resolved himself to further negotiations at Newport on the Isle of Wight; to which, with a vote of 129 to 83, Parliament agreed. Cromwell however, was having none of it, stating that a permanent peace was impossible while Charles lived, and opposed any further talks with someone both he and the army, (according to him anyway) viewed as a tyrant, and who were already taking steps to consolidate their power with a Parliamentary purge. On the 6th and 7th of December 1648, any members of Parliament who were deemed unsympathetic to the military were either arrested or excluded while others chose to stay out of harm's way voluntarily! The ones that were left formed a "Rump Parliament", which was the remnants, or literally "arse end", of a previously constitutional one, making this to all intents and purposes, a military coup and were to result in the king's trial for treason and subsequent execution. This rump Parliament established a high court of justice in early January 1649.

On the 20th of that month Charles was charged with "high treason against the realm of England"! The King not only refuted the charge but also refused to plead saying he did not recognise the legality of the high court as it had been established by a commons purged of any dissent and was also rejected by the House of Lords. The concept of trying a King was a novel one and the Chief Justices of the three common law courts of England, all opposed the indictment as being unlawful. In reply, the rump Parliament declared they were capable of legislating alone and passed a bill creating a separate court for Charles's trial. The said bill was also declared an act and therefore had no need for royal assent! The court established by this act consisted of 135 commissioners but only 68 of them, all firm Parliamentarians, actually attended the trial where John Bradshaw acted as President of the Court and the prosecution was led by the Solicitor General, John Cook

During the first three days of the trial whenever Charles was asked to plead, he refused, stating that he did not recognise this court and that no court had jurisdiction over a monarch anyway.

He also declared that his own authority to rule had been God granted and that the power being wielded by those trying him was only that of force of arms and the trial therefore was illegal. By contrast, the court challenged the doctrine of sovereign immunity, stating that the King of England was not a person, but an office, which was entrusted with a limited power to govern by, and according to, the laws of the land. At the end of the third day Charles was removed from court, which then heard the case for the prosecution over the next two days and duly condemned him to death on the 26th. On the 27th, the King was brought in, declared guilty and sentenced. Fifty nine of the commissioners signed the death warrant! The decapitation was set for the morning of Tuesday the 30th of January 1649 and on that morning the King called for two shirts to wear as the weather was inclement and chilly and he did not want anyone to mistake any involuntary shivers by him as a sign of fear, Charles thus displayed the same courage and resolve in the face of death that his Grandmother, Mary Queen of Scots, had displayed before him! He was executed on a scaffold which had been erected in front of the Banqueting House of the Palace of Whitehall.

On the day after the execution, the King's head was sewn back onto his body, by permission of Cromwell, and he was then embalmed and placed in a lead coffin. The commission had refused permission for him to be buried at Westminster Abbey, and he was interred instead at Windsor in a vault beside Henry VIII. The same day as his execution, an act was passed by the rump parliament forbidding the proclamation of another monarch thus denying Charles II his right of automatic succession. With the monarchy thus overthrown, and the House of Lords simultaneously abolished, England became a republic or "Commonwealth" and on the 7th of February 1649 the office of King was formally abolished in England! Cromwell was later to forcibly disband the rump parliament in 1653 thereby establishing a protectorate with himself as the "Lord Protector". This actually made him "King" in all but name and without a doubt pandered to the ego of this anti-monarchist, Puritan extremist!

Thus ended the reign of the tenth monarch of the Stewart dynasty, a controversial reign by a controversial monarch and in a very controversial manner! It also brought to an end, temporarily at least, the actual dynasty itself, causing all sorts of problems throughout the three Kingdoms in the process! Charles, that staunch believer in the "Divine Right of Kings", was actually martyred by the Church of England at his death and was canonised by them after the Reformation, becoming known as "St Charles, King and Martyr" (Anglican), the one and only Saint of that Church!

The Interregnum, 1649 – 1660

Although an Interregnum was declared in England and Ireland virtually from the moment of Charles I's death on the 30th of January 1649, this was not the case in Scotland, who's Covenanter Parliament honoured the automatic succession and recognised Charles II as King of Scotland from that same date! They then chose to honour existing protocol and proclaimed Charles II King of Great Britain, France and Ireland at the Mercat Cross in Edinburgh six days later on the 5th of February 1649, even though the English parliament passed a statute making any such proclamation unlawful! Charles's coronation as King of Scotland took place on the 1st of January 1651 at Scone, which was the last coronation to be held there, but his reign was to be short lived as he fled the British Isles into a nine year long, self-imposed exile abroad, when an ill-fated and ill-advised invasion of England collapsed after a comprehensive defeat at the hands of Cromwell and the New Model Army at the Battle of Worcester on the 3rd of September 1651. After this Scotland was governed by the military which lasted, as with the rest of the country, until the Restoration of the Monarchy on the 29th of May 1660! So, although the interregnum was a *De Facto* state in England and Ireland, it did not exist in Scotland, who's recognised and Crowned Monarch was *in absentia* abroad for nine years. Although this period tends to be known as the "Third English Civil War 1649 – 1651", it was in fact more of a Scotland V England confrontation with the English Parliamentarians having the final say at Worcester in 1651!

The execution of Charles I in January 1649 ushered in this period known as the interregnum and it ended in July 1660 when his son, Charles II, was restored, by invitation, to the thrones of the three Kingdoms although he had already been acclaimed King in Scotland since 1651. The precise start and end of this period and the social and political events which occurred during it, varied considerably across the three Kingdoms. Scotland's unilateral recognition of Charles II for instance, prompted a swift retaliation from the English Parliamentarians and an Army under Cromwell gave a Scottish Covenanter Army a decisive beating at the Battle of Dunbar on the 3rd of September 1650 which was followed up by another one at Worcester a year later, so dispelling any lingering doubts that Cromwell and his Parliamentarian Roundheads were in overall charge of things throughout the country as a whole.

This retaliation may well have been even swifter but for the fact that Cromwell had been busy elsewhere bringing to an end the Irish Confederate Wars. He had personally fronted a bloody campaign in Ireland from the August of 1649 to the May of 1650 when he had left for Scotland, but his brutal work carried on unabated in his absence until 1653! Roughly one third of Ireland's Catholic population were killed or exiled during this genocidal purge, famine and plague being the biggest culprits and these resulted from a deliberate "scorched earth" policy by the Parliamentarians; some of the Irish prisoners of war were sold into indentured slavery in the West Indies! The practice of Catholicism was banned and this gave birth to soldiers and settlers setting up religious communities of Quakers and Baptists and the like under the protection of the Parliamentary forces. A "softening" of these policies started happening with the introduction of Cromwell's fourth son, Henry, who replaced Charles Fleetwood as Parliamentary commander in 1655 and under him, the Parliamentary Generals

Charles Coote and Richard Boyle started occupying the more strategic points in the country in preparation for the coming Restoration. Before Henry Cromwell's intervention, Catholics had even been banned from living in towns!

Back in Scotland on the 28th of October 1651, a declaration known as the "Tender of Union" was made by the English rump parliament to the effect that Scotland would cease to have its own parliament and would join with the English in its emerging "Commonwealth" Republic! A proclamation to this effect was made at the Mercat Cross in Edinburgh on the 4th of February 1652. Two years later on the 12th of April 1654, the *Ordinance for Uniting Scotland into one Commonwealth with England*" was issued by the Lord Protector, Oliver Cromwell, and was proclaimed by the military governor of Scotland, General George Monck. This ordinance did not become an Act of Union until its approval by the Secondary Protectorate Parliament on the 26th of June 1657. The reason that it took so long was that parliaments were dissolving almost as quickly as they were being created; this act ran out of time progressively in the "rump parliament", the "barebones parliament" and then the "first protectorate parliament" before finally passing in the second one!

A final Royalist uprising took place in the Highlands during 1653 to 1655 and was led by William Cunningham, 9th Earl of Glencairn and John Middleton, 1st Earl of Middleton, veterans of the earlier Royalist causes with both Charles and his son, Charles II. After some initial successes it suffered from internal divisions and eventually fell apart after a heavy defeat at the battle of Dalnaspidal on the 19th of July 1654. Here the Clans McGregor and Robertson fought with the Royalists while the Clan Campbell, under Archibald Campbell, 1st Marquess of Argyll and Sir Thomas Morgan, an aide to General George Monck, led the Parliamentary Army loyal to Cromwell. Morgan was later to aid Monck in his march south to facilitate the Restoration in 1660.

Cromwell's subjugation of Scotland during the rule of the Commonwealth 1651 to 1654, and later, the Protectorate from 1655 on, was largely peaceful, mainly due to the fact that there were no wholesale confiscations of land or property plus the country was jointly governed by a Scottish Council of State as well as the Parliamentary military authorities. This situation, unwelcome as it was, and rarely favourably viewed, did not however, incite the lasting hatred there that the very mention of his name does in Ireland, even to this day!

The Interregnum in England saw no less than seven different parliaments created and subsequently dissolved during its twelve year existence! When the Church of England was disestablished by the Commonwealth Government, the question of what to replace it with became a hotly debated, and disputed, subject and in the end it became impossible to satisfy, far less appease, the many and diverse political and religious factions. During this time Cromwell lost much of the support he had gained during the Civil Wars and was becoming increasingly unpopular with the now mostly Puritan based rank and file, this was due in part at least to his perceived failure to abolish the aristocracy. The result of all this was that when Cromwell died of an illness related to a kidney infection on the 3rd of September 1658, few people throughout Britain went into deep mourning for him. Unlike his arch protagonist Charles I who was sanctified in death, Poor Oliver was demonised! On the 12th anniversary of Charles's execution, the 30th of January 1661, Cromwell's body was exhumed and subjected to the ritual of posthumous execution, it was then hung in chains at Tyburn and the decapitated body flung unceremoniously into a pit! The head is allegedly buried in an undisclosed spot under the floor of his old antechamber at Cambridge College!

The general feeling of antipathy towards Richard Cromwell intensified when it quickly became obvious that the son and successor, though not without ability, was anything but a chip off the old block. The son had no power base in either the army or political circles and was duly forced to resign in May 1659, thus ending the Protectorate.   This left no clear leadership among the many factions who now jostled for power during the reinstated and short lived Commonwealth, and in fact, cleared the way for General Monck, Military Governor of Scotland and head of the New Model Army there, to make his initial moves which culminated with the Restoration of Charles II!   Monck had been gainfully employed as a General-at-Sea from 1652 but in early 1655 returned to his Scottish command after the uprising of Glencairn had been put down whereupon he proceeded to purge his own troops of moderates, Quakers and other such radicals.

He supervised the construction of the great Cromwellian Citadels at Ayr, Perth and Leith as well as the twenty or so smaller forts across the country and as far out as Orkney and Stornoway. He also imposed law and order in the Highlands by making the Clan Chiefs responsible for keeping the peace in their own areas. In spite of rumours to the contrary, Monck stayed on friendly terms with Cromwell and remained loyal to the Protectorate. On Oliver's death 1658 he declared his allegiance to Richard but, on receiving no appeal for help from him on his resignation in May 1659, declared his allegiance, and that of the army in Scotland, to Parliament instead. He was now approached by Royalist representatives regarding a possible restoration of the monarchy but refused to commit himself either way at this stage in the proceedings.

In October 1659 he stated that he would uphold parliament's authority when Sir Arthur Heselrige appealed for support against the Council of officer's forcible dissolution of parliament, which Monck regarded as a radical step too far and which threatened not only the Church but also his own moderate Presbyterianism. He maintained his control over the army in Scotland by sending out a task force of loyal soldiers around the many garrisons to arrest unreliable officers; around a hundred or so were purged by these means and were replaced with tried and trusted men loyal to Monck! Meanwhile, a leading member of the military junta, Major general Lambert, was marching north to confront Monck and he reached as far as Newcastle by mid-November 1659 but, faced with severe weather conditions and a lack of pay, his troops began to desert. The leaders of the deeply unpopular Junta in London were finally obliged to step down when Vice Admiral Lawson threatened to blockade the port in the December of that year. The Commonwealth was thus restored and General Monck was subsequently declared commander-in-chief of all land forces in England and Scotland!

At parliament's invitation, Monck marched south at the head of 5,000 foot and 2,000 horse, crossing the border at Coldstream on the 1st of January 1660, the remnants of Lambert's army disintegrating before his advance. He forestalled the possibility of any organised opposition in London by demanding that the regiments already stationed there should be dispersed to garrisons' out with the city to make way for his own troops. He occupied the capital on the 3rd of February and, recognising the deep unpopularity of the rump parliament, called for the re-admission of MP's purged from it in 1648. This was a shrewd move and was met with great acclaim by the people! Although continuing to proclaim his support for the commonwealth in public, Monck also entered into secret negotiations with the representatives of Charles Stewart during March and these resulted in the Declaration of Breda by the Stewart exile. The restored Long Parliament in the meantime, voted to dissolve itself on the 16th of March and to call for new elections. Subsequently the pro-Royalist Convention Parliament duly assembled on the 25th of April 1660 and the Restoration became inevitable!

Charles Stewart, King Charles II, 1660 – 1685

As the restored King landed at Dover on the 25th of May 1660, General Monck was the first to greet him as he stepped ashore; receiving the investiture of the Order of the Garter the following day for his troubles! Amongst other honours for his part in the restoration, he was appointed Captain-General of the army and created Earl of Torrington and Duke of Albemarle. Monck's own "Regiment of Foot" – originally formed by Cromwell in 1650 – was the only New Model Army regiment to be incorporated into Charles II's standing army, where it became known, and still is today, as the "Coldstream Guards"! A troop of Monck's cavalry regiment was also incorporated into the Royal Horse Guards (becoming the Blues and Royals) and these are the only two regiments in the British Army today who can trace their roots back to Cromwell's New Model Army, which was subsequently disbanded in this the year of the Restoration of the Monarchy, 1660!

Anyway, enough of Monck, the Interregnum and the Restoration, this is after all, about the Stewarts and their dynasty, and we will take up where we left off here, after Charles I's execution in 1649, with the reign of Charles II which actually started officially on the 29th of May, four days after his return from exile at Dover on the 25th. After his restoration, all legal documents were dated as if he had succeeded his father as King in 1649! He reigned until his death on the 6th of February 1685 when he was succeeded by his younger brother, James VII & II, as he had died without legitimate issue! This was not to say he had no children, he just hadn't had them by his wife, Catherine of Braganza! He is credited with fourteen known illegitimate children by seven known mistresses and possibly several other offspring by another six suspected mistresses so, like his ancestor Robert II, he went quite a ways to repopulating the earth, or at least his local part of it anyway! The King was sometimes nicknamed "Old Rowley", after a prolific breeding stallion in his stables!

Charles II had been born in St. James's Palace on the 29th of May 1630 to parents who were Charles I, King of Scotland, England and Ireland, and his Queen, Henrietta Maria, a sister of the French King Louis XIII. These three kingdoms were respectively, and predominately, Presbyterian, Episcopalian and Roman Catholic in turn. Charles's Protestant baptism was in the Chapel Royal on the 27th of June and was officiated over by the Anglican Bishop of London, William Laud. He was raised in the care of the Protestant Countess of Dorset though his Godparents were both Catholic. At his birth he automatically became the Dukes of both Rothesay and Cornwall and at age eight, he was designated Prince of Wales although he was never formally invested with this honour.

The young Prince accompanied his father in his campaigns of the 1640's but by 1646 Charles I was losing the wars and his son left England due to fears for his safety. After England became a republic with Charles's decapitation in January 1649, the Covenanter parliament of Scotland proclaimed Charles II King of Great Britain, France and Ireland at the Mercat Cross in Edinburgh but refused him entry to Scotland unless he accepted Presbyterianism throughout Britain and Ireland by supporting the Solemn League and Covenant. When he eventually arrived in Scotland on the 23rd of June 1650 it was under those terms and, in addition, he formally had to agree to the Covenant and to his abandonment of Episcopal Church government which was fine in Scotland but made him unpopular in the republic of England. The young King came to despise the hypocrisy and villainy of the Covenanters!

Charles was crowned on the 23rd of April 1661 at Westminster Abbey, thereby adding the English and Irish Crowns – the Irish had declared Charles for King at a convention on the 14th of May1660 - to the Scottish one he had already worn since the 1st of January 1651 at Scone, despite being in exile for nine years; thus a Stewart once again ruled over the three Kingdoms of Scotland, England and Ireland. He became popularly known as the "Merry Monarch", due in part to the liveliness and hedonism of his court (to say nothing of his own lifestyle) but also to the general relief felt at the return to normality after almost twelve years of a harsh Puritanical and Calvinistic rule by Cromwell and his adherents. This had been particularly brutal in Ireland and even now, Charles's government was still unwilling to tolerate Catholicism there but instead, were focusing on trying to establish an Episcopalian styled Protestant Church!

On the 4th of April 1660, prior to his return to British soil Charles had issued his "Declaration of Breda", this was a proclamation by which he promised a general pardon for crimes committed during the English civil wars, and the interregnum, to all those who were now willing to recognise him as their lawful King. On the 8th of May, whilst still at Breda, Charles received the invitation to return to London and take up his rightful position as King; he subsequently landed at Dover on the 25th, entered London on the 28th and resumed the monarchy on the 29th, being formally crowned on the 23rd of April 1661!

His Declaration of Breda went much further than just being a general, all encompassing pardon, it also stated retention for the present owners of property purchased during that same period, religious toleration for all, payment of arrears due to the army and that the New Model Army would be recommissioned into service under the crown! Further emphasis and clarification on these points were added by the "Indemnity and Oblivion Act" of the 29th of August 1660, this specifically stated that Charles pardon all those involved in the regicide of his father except for those directly involved in his execution who numbered fifty! Nine of these were hung, drawn and quartered; others were given life imprisonment, which in these days was no joke, whilst others were simply excluded from office for life. Poor old Oliver was dug up and decapitated for his part in the proceedings!

By the same act, the lands of the Crown and the established Church were to be automatically restored but the lands of Royalists and other dissenters, confiscated and sold during that period, were to be left for private negotiation or litigation which meant that loyalists could expect no government help in regaining what had once been theirs! This understandably angered and disappointed a lot of people who saw the act as indemnity for Charles's enemies and oblivion for his friends. The passage of this act through the Convention Parliament of the day was secured by Lord Clarendon, Charles's first minister, and which was duly dissolved in the December of that year to be replaced by the "Cavalier Parliament" in early 1661. This parliament was overwhelmingly Royalist and Anglican and spared no pains in ensuring the total dominance of these aspects with the following acts!

The "Corporation Act" of 1661 required municipal office bearers to swear allegiance, the "Act of Uniformity" of 1662 made the use of the Anglican Book of Common Prayer compulsory, the "Conventicle Act" of 1664 prohibited religious assemblies of more than five people (except for C of E) and the "Five Mile Act" of 1665 prohibited expelled non-conforming clergymen from coming within a five mile radius of a parish from which they had been banished! These last two remained in effect for the remainder of Charles's reign and the four of them combined were known as the "Clarendon Code" even though he was not directly responsible for them and had even been vociferous against the five mile act. So much then, for the "Religious Tolerance" in Charles's "Declaration of Breda" of April 1660!

The Restoration in general was accompanied by a vast social change; one could almost go as far as to say a lowering, or in some cases, a plummeting, of moral standards! Puritanism had lost its momentum and the theatres, closed by Cromwell, reopened to stage bawdy "Restoration Comedy" which became a recognisable genre of the time! A marriage contract between Charles and Catherine of Braganza which had been signed on the 23rd of June 1661 was finally honoured when the couple were married on the 21st of May 1662, in two ceremonies! Firstly in a secret Catholic one and then in a public, Anglican one! Catherine being Catholic and Portuguese, it goes without saying that the match was not a popular one, even though her dowry brought both Tangiers and Bombay under British control as well as giving trading privileges in Brazil and the East Indies.

257

Unfortunately for the lady but not so for the monarchy, Catherine had four pregnancies but sadly produced no children, this however, didn't stop Charles in his prolific fathering of bastards elsewhere and by several other mistresses, known and unknown! Also in 1662, an unpopular move by Charles saw the sale Of Dunkirk to his first cousin King Louis XIV of France for almost half a million pounds sterling. This channel port, although valuable strategically, had nonetheless been a drain on Charles's limited finances despite them being boosted by about £300,000 in a cash settlement with his marriage to Catherine.

The Dutch War of 1665 to 1667 was started by British attempts to muscle in on Dutch territories in North Africa and America. The conflict began well for Britain with the capture of New Amsterdam and its subsequent renaming to New York, in honour of Charles's younger brother James, then Duke of York! This was followed by, and emphasised with, a decisive victory for the English fleet at the Battle of Lowestoft, which lasted four days beginning on the 13th of June 1665 and where the Dutch fleet lost 17 ships of the line out of a fleet of 103 against England's single casualty out of a fleet of 109; the English were commanded by James, Duke of York. The

Dutch however, were to get their own back, and more, at the "Raid on the Medway" in June 1667 when they bombarded and captured Sheerness, sailed up the river Thames to Gravesend, then up the river Medway to Chatham and proceeded to set about the English fleet laid up there!

They torched three capital ships; ten lesser vessels then captured and towed away the *Unity* and the English Flagship, *Royal Charles* which were taken back to the Netherlands as trophies! This was the biggest and most humiliating defeat ever suffered by the Royal Navy and one of the worst disasters ever suffered by the British military generally. The war ended shortly after this, unsurprisingly, with the signing of the Treaty of Breda! (As opposed to Charles's declaration of Breda) This little escapade did, however, put paid to the popular myth that England had never been invaded by a foreign power since 1066! Then of course there's always the "Glorious Revolution" (those Dutch again) in 1688 and the Scots in 1513!

Two other great historical events happened in Charles's London, or should I say "to" Charles's London during this war, the first was the Great Plague of 1665 - which was reminiscent of a similar disaster in Scotland in 1350 – and during which some 60,000 people lost their lives; 7,000 in one week alone at the peak! All attempts by the London health officials to contain the disease failed miserably and who knows what would have happened if the second disaster, which actually proved to be a blessing in disguise, hadn't come along on the 2nd of September 1666; the Great Fire! This consumed over 13,000 houses and 80 odd churches including St. Paul's Cathedral and was originally attributed to Catholic conspirators although it was later found to have been started accidentally in a bakery in Pudding Lane! The King and his brother James, having been lambasted for fleeing the capital in the face of the plague, earned many plaudits and redeemed themselves here for joining in and directing the fire-fighting efforts of the ordinary public during the conflagration; Sir Christopher Wren was commissioned to redesign and rebuild St. Paul's.

In 1667 Charles saw fit to dismiss his Lord Chancellor, Clarendon, an advisor from his days of exile, using him as a scapegoat for the Dutch War and the disaster of the Medway. Lord Clarendon was replaced with a "cabal", an acronym for Clifford, Ashley, Buckingham, Arlington and Lauderdale; these however, rarely acted in concert and were usually split into two factions led by Arlington and Buckingham, with

Arlington the more successful of the two. Clifford and Arlington however, were both secret Catholics! Clarendon's daughter Anne was the first wife of Charles's brother James and the mother of both Stewart monarchs, Queen Mary II and Queen Anne!

Charles allied himself with Sweden and his former enemy, the Netherlands, in 1668 to Oppose Louis XIV in the War of Devolution, a fairly minor confrontation between France and Spain over possession of the Spanish Netherlands, which then were the present-day Belgium and Luxembourg. By 1669 Louis had made peace with this triple alliance but maintained his aggression towards the Dutch Netherlands. In 1670 Charles sought to solve his financial problems by agreeing to a secret Treaty of Dover with France; under this, Louis agreed to pay Charles £160,000 each year in return for his conversion for to Catholicism, the re-establishing of Catholicism in England and support for the French King's projected war with the Dutch! Charles endeavoured to ensure that this treaty, and in particular his conversion clause, remained a top secret and it is questionable, at this point at least, if he ever really intended to convert although he eventually did so on his death-bed in 1685! He did however; issue a "Declaration of

Indulgence" using his prerogative powers, to suspend the penal laws against Catholics and non-conformists. In the event, he was forced to withdraw this declaration in 1673 due to fierce opposition from the Anglican parliament.

As Charles's unfortunate wife, Queen Catherine had been unable to produce an heir, her four pregnancies ending in either miscarriages or stillbirths in 1662, 1666, 1668 and 1669; Charles's heir presumptive was therefore his unpopular and Catholic brother James, Duke of York. To assuage public fears that the royal family was too Catholic, Charles agreed that his Protestant niece, James's daughter Mary, should marry the Protestant William of Orange. This was to restore the balance after his brother's second Marriage to the Catholic Mary of Modena and to re-establish his own Protestant credentials at the same time. Religious intolerance and Anti-Catholicism was widespread! The "Test Act" of 1673 excluded Roman Catholics from both houses of parliament, the principle being that none but those taking communion in the established Anglican Church were eligible, or fit for public employment!

By 1678 this intolerance had escalated into hysteria, agitated by one Titus Oates who had alternatively been an Anglican and Jesuit priest and who was advocating the existence of a fiendish "Popish Plot" to assassinate the King; even accusing his Queen of complicity. Charles did not believe these allegations but ordered his chief minister, Lord Danby (also accused) to investigate. While Danby seems to have been rightly sceptical about Oates and his claims, the Cavalier parliament was not! Judges and Juries across the land condemned the supposed conspirators, resulting in numerous innocent individuals being executed on little or no evidence! The parliament impeached Lord Danby and presented a bill to exclude James from the succession. To save Danby from impeachment and his brother from exclusion, Charles dissolved the Cavalier parliament in January 1679, declaring that he would no longer tolerate any talk of a change of succession!

The new "Habeas Corpus" parliament which met two months later was quite hostile to Charles as many of its members felt he intended to use the standing army to either suppress dissent, or to impose Catholicism, possibly both! The reality of the matter was that with insufficient funds voted by parliament, Charles was forced to gradually disband his troops. Lord Danby in the meantime, had resigned his post as Lord High Treasurer having lost parliamentary support on the one hand, but on the other, receiving a pardon from the King. In open defiance of the royal will, the Commons declared that the dissolution of parliament did not interrupt impeachment proceedings and that the pardon was therefore invalid. When the Lords attempted to impose the punishment of exile – which the Commons thought too mild – the impeachment became stalled between the two Houses. As had been required of him so many times before during his reign; Charles bowed to the wishes of his protagonists and committed Danby to the Tower of London, where he was to spend the next five years of his life.

Charles now faced a political storm over the succession to the throne as the prospect of a Catholic monarch was vehemently opposed by many, particularly the Earl of Shaftesbury who was previously Baron Ashley and a member of the "cabal". His power was strengthened when the Commons of 1679 introduced the "Exclusion Bill", the purpose of which was obviously to exclude the Duke of York from the line of succession; some even sought to replace him with the Protestant Duke of Monmouth, the eldest of Charles's bastards! All this gave birth to two new factions in the House, the *"Abhorrers"* and the "*Petitioners*"! The former – those who thought the Bill abhorrent – were named "*Tories*" (after a term for disposed Irish Catholic bandits) while the latter – those who supported the Bill – were called "*Whigs*" (after a term for rebellious Scottish Presbyterians). Both of these were terms of abuse! Charles, fearing that the Exclusion Bill would be passed, dissolved the Habeas Corpus parliament on the 12th of July 1679.

Charles's hopes for a more moderate parliament were again frustrated and within a few months, on the 18th of January 1681, he dissolved the "Exclusion Bill" parliament after it had sought to pass that very Bill! A new parliament, the "Oxford Parliament", was formed two days later and which was again dissolved by Charles, at Oxford, just two months later and for the remainder of his reign Charles ruled without a Parliament. Support for the Bill however, ebbed during the early '80's and Charles enjoyed a nationwide surge of loyalty. Shaftesbury was unsuccessfully prosecuted for treason in 1681, and fearing a repeat in 1682, fled the country to the Dutch Netherlands and the Court of William of Orange where he died of ill health in January 1683.

The King's opposition to the Exclusion Bill had angered a lot of Protestants and some of them conspired to formulate the "Rye House Plot" of April 1683 which was a plan to murder the King and the Duke of York as they returned from the Newmarket races to London. A fire however, destroyed their lodgings in Newmarket forcing them to leave early and thus, inadvertently, avoiding the planned ambush but news of the failed plot was leaked! Protestant leaders and politicians such as Sir Arthur Capell the 1st Earl of Essex, Algernon Sydney, Lord William Russell and the Duke of Monmouth were all implicated. Essex slit his own throat whilst imprisoned in the Tower of London, Sydney and Russell were both executed for high treason and Monmouth followed in Shaftesbury's footsteps, fleeing for safety to the Court of William of Orange in Holland. Danby and other Catholic Lords were released from the Tower; Titus Oates was convicted and flung into it and the Duke of York acquired a greater influence and more respect at Court!

Charles suffered a sudden and serious apoplectic fit on the morning of the 2nd of February 1685 and died at 11.45 am four days later at the Palace of Whitehall. He was 54 years old. The suddenness of this immediately raised the spectre of poison but modern medicine has since decided that his symptoms were due to Uraemia or kidney dysfunction. On his deathbed he not only asked his brother James to look after his mistresses but was also received into the Catholic Church thereby keeping his long-standing promise to the French King! He was buried in Westminster Abbey without undue ceremony!

James Stewart, King James VII & II, 1685 – 1688

James, the twelfth monarch of the dynasty, and the last male one - King William who came after him wasn't truly a Stewart – ascended to the throne on the death of his brother on the 6th of February 1685 and reigned until his abdication / deposition on the 11th of December 1688. Like his brother and predecessor Charles II, James, who was born on the 14th of October 1633, was also baptised a Protestant but chose to take the Catholic Eucharist sometime in 1668 0r '69. He made his conversion public knowledge some five years later with his deliberate failure to recognise the "Test Act" of 1673. He was thus the first Roman Catholic monarch since his great grandmother Mary, Queen of Scots and he was also the last Catholic to reign over the Kingdoms of Scotland, England and Ireland! Already the Duke of York in England from birth, he was created Duke of Albany in Scotland by his brother, the King, after the restoration of the monarchy in 1660.

On that subject, before we have a look at James's life and escapades, I have decided at this point to clarify his marriages and the subsequent succession to the throne as this becomes increasingly complicated as we progress: being decided by various criteria not the least important of which by far, was religion! His first marriage was to Anne Hyde on the 3rd of September 1660 who was the Anglican daughter of a lawyer and commoner called Edward Hyde. Hyde was quickly elevated to the peerage after his daughter's wedding, within two months to be exact, by Charles II, as Baron Hyde – it just wouldn't do to have commoners in the family after all - then to the Earl of Clarendon in 1661! After her marriage, Anne automatically became the Duchess's of Albany and York and she also converted to Catholicism sometime around 1661, after exposure to that religion on earlier European trips, James was to follow suit after a few years. Anne unfortunately died of cancer in 1671.

The couple had eight children but only two of them were to survive, the rest dying in infancy. These were Mary, born on the 30th of April 1662, the future Queen Mary II of the three Kingdoms and wife of King William of Orange; and Anne, born on the 6th of February 1665 and the future

Queen Anne of Great Britain and Ireland. Both of these ladies were born, and remained, on the orders of their uncle King Charles II, Protestants! James's second marriage on the 23rd of November 1673 was to the Catholic Mary of Modena, from the north-western Italian Duchy of Modena and this is what led to, in modern day parlance, the shit really hitting the fan! Now a Catholic himself, James and Mary had five children, three of whom died as infants. Two others, both daughters reached age five and twenty respectively. But the catalyst, the explosion which rent asunder all pretence of dignified succession, came on the 10th of June 1688 with the birth of one James Francis Edward Stewart, who became heir to the throne as the future James VIII & III, a son, and a Catholic! He was looked upon by the Anglican parliamentary hierarchy as the anti-Christ, and the situation was likened to Armageddon!

The staunchly Anglican English establishment and the mostly Protestant nobility, was not about to allow this to happen. They already had a monarch who was Catholic "by the back door" as they saw it and there was no way they were going to tolerate a "legitimate" one ascending the throne and thereby once again re-establishing a Catholic line of succession for the

Royal House of Stewart! Until the 10th of June 1688, the heir presumptive for the thrones of Scotland, England and Ireland had been Mary, James's eldest surviving daughter who had married William III, Prince of Orange in St James's Palace on the 4th of November 1677, Henry Compton, Bishop of London and one of the "immortal seven" eleven years later, officiating! William and Mary, as they became known, were first cousins, both Protestant and shared a common grandfather in King Charles I.

On the 30th of June 1688 (they hadn't lost much time) Prince William received a letter from the "immortal seven" inviting him "to depose the Catholic King James by the invasion of England"! These seven, the Earls of Danby, Shrewsbury, Devonshire and Oxford, Viscounts Lumley and Sydney – who was the author of the letter – and the Bishop of London, Henry Compton, had taken it upon themselves, with the blessing of almost everyone else who mattered in England, to take this particular bull by the horns and set in motion what was to become known as the "Glorious Revolution"! This was to be the effective overthrow of the Catholic King James II of England and Ireland (James VII of Scotland), by a union of English Parliamentarians and the Dutch Stadtholder William III of Orange-Nassau.

William's successful, and virtually bloodless, invasion with a Dutch fleet and army at Torbay in the November met with little or no resistance and culminated with him ascending the throne as King William III of England and Ireland (William II of Scotland) along with his wife Queen Mary II of Scotland, England and Ireland!

William convinced a newly chosen "Convention Parliament" to make him and his wife joint rulers on the 13th of February 1689, by which time James had long since flown the coop to France, throwing the Great Seal of England into the Thames as he went, these actions by him were seen by the country to be a legal statement of Abdication as of the 11th of December1688! The momentous events of that year had the effect of kick-starting a period of Catholic persecution country wide which was to last for over a hundred years and cause a lot of grief along the way. King James's earlier policy of tolerance for Roman Catholics and Protestant non-conformists, which played a big part in his downfall, was now sorely missed! The whole crux of the matter was of course, not so much his conversion to Catholicism, but his publicising the fact by disrespecting the "Test Act" of 1673 which required him to make a declaration of affinity to Anglicism and thereby disavowing the

Church of Rome including the invocation of Saints and the sacrament of Mass! All this resulted not only in James's abdication but also the passage of the Bill of Rights and the eventual Hanoverian succession!

To regress to early 1685, and despite his policy of religious toleration in England, James pursued a totally different one in Scotland, here he continued with his brother's policy of the merciless persecution of the Presbyterian Covenanters! Charles II had elected John Maitland, the Earl of Lauderdale and a later member of the "cabal" government, as Secretary of State for Scotland in May 1660 and gave him *carte-blanche* to run the country as he saw fit, Charles wanting no part of it! Maitland, originally a Presbyterian and Covenanter himself, by 1669 and for his own ends, had swung full circle and become an Episcopalian, wilfully and actively overseeing its establishment and the subsequent downfall of Presbyterianism, thereby giving rise to the creation of "conventicles" – an outlawed form of open-air worship often raided by government troops and causing much loss of life – and which became known as the "killing times", a period roughly covering 1680 to 1688! Organised resistance by the Presbyterian Covenanters had collapsed with a heavy defeat at the Battle of Bothwell Brig on the 22nd of June 1679 by government troops led by James Scott, 1st Duke of Monmouth and John Graham of Claverhouse, 1st Viscount of Dundee!

Soon after occupying the throne, James found himself with two rebellions to deal with, the first was in the south west of England and led by his nephew James Scott, the 1st Duke of Monmouth, while the second was in Scotland and led by Archibald Campbell, the Earl of Argyll. Both these men had begun their expeditions from Holland where James's nephew and son-in-law, William of Orange, had neglected to detain them or put a stop to their recruitment efforts. Argyll sailed to Scotland with fewer than 300men and on arrival there attempted to raise more recruits, but not enough, mainly from his own clan, the Campbell's, and the insurrection quickly fizzled out. He had never posed a serious threat to James and was himself captured at Inchinnan on the 18th of June 1685 and taken to Edinburgh as a prisoner. A new trial was not instigated because Argyll had previously been tried and sentenced to death for prior misdemeanours against the Crown. The King confirmed this earlier sentence and ordered that it be carried out, post-haste!

Monmouth's rebellion had been co-ordinated with Argyll's but the former was far more dangerous to James as he had proclaimed himself King at Lyme Regis on the 11th of June by virtue of his being the eldest of Charles II's bastard sons! Like Argyll, he had difficulty in recruiting and was unable to get enough men to pose a serious threat to even the small standing army at James's disposal. Looking to gain every possible advantage, Monmouth had mounted his attack at the Battle of Sedgemoor, 6th of July 1685, on the King's forces at 10 o'clock at night but failed to take advantage of the element of surprise as the Royalist's were far superior in training and organisation than the rebel's. They were led by the Duke of Marlborough, the Duke of Grafton and the Earl of Feversham and their forces consisted of 500 men of the 1st Regiment of Foot (the Royal Scots) and 600 men of the 2nd Regiment of Guards (Coldstream Guards) amongst many others.

It was virtually a walkover for the Royalists and Monmouth himself was captured after escaping from the battlefield, and taken to London for trial and execution. This was presumably in the days before a man was deemed innocent until proven guilty! These trials became known as the "Bloody Assizes" and were presided over by the notorious Judge Jeffries who condemned many of the rebels to transportation and indentured servitude in the West Indies as well as having 250 of the ringleaders executed by drawing and quartering! Jeffries allegedly browbeat witnesses and jurors, cursed his victims and gloated over them, giving guilt the benefit of every doubt except where a substantial bribe had been paid! James did make some effort to check the brutality but later raised Jeffries to the peerage and made him Lord Chancellor on the 6th of September 1686. Both rebellions were easily enough defeated but only served to harden James's resolve against his enemies and grossly magnified his suspicion of the Dutch, with good reason as it was to later prove!

To protect himself from further rebellions, James sought the safety of an enlarged standing army. This alarmed many of his subjects, not only because of the trouble soldiers caused in the towns, but because it was against the English tradition to keep a professional army in peacetime. Even more alarming to Parliament was James's use of his dispensing power to allow Roman Catholics to command several regiments without having to take the oath mandated by the Test Act! When even the previously supportive Parliament objected to these measures, James ordered Parliament prorogued – which means suspended, not dissolved – in the November 1685 and it was never to meet again in his reign. In the beginning of 1686 two papers were found in Charles II's strong box in his private closet, in his own hand, stating the arguments for Catholicism over Protestantism. James published these papers with a declaration signed by him and challenged the Archbishop of Canterbury, and the whole Anglican Episcopalian bench to refute Charles's arguments: "Let me have a solid answer, and in a gentlemanlike style" he said, "and it may have the effect which you so much desire of bringing me over to your church". The Archbishop refused to answer on the grounds of respect for the late king!

James advocated for the repeal of the penal laws in all three of his kingdoms, but in the early years of his reign he refused to allow those dissenters who did not petition for this relief to receive it. Running true to form as far as Scotland went, James sent a letter to the Scottish Parliament at its opening in 1685, declaring his wish for new penal laws against the stubborn and rebellious Presbyterians and lamented that he was not there in person to promote such a law! In response, the Parliament passed an Act that stated, "Whoever should preach in a conventicle under a roof, or should attend, either as preacher or as a hearer, a conventicle in the open air should be punished with death and confiscation of property"! In March 1686, James sent a letter to the Scottish Privy Council advocating toleration for Catholics but that the persecution of the Presbyterian Covenanters should continue, calling them to London when they refused to acquiesce to his wishes. Once there, the Privy Councilors explained that they would grant relief to Catholics only if a similar relief was provided for the Covenanters and if James promised not to attempt anything that would harm the Protestant religion. James agreed to a degree of relief to Presbyterians, but not to the full toleration he wanted for Catholics, declaring that the Protestant religion was false and that he would not promise not to prejudice a false religion!

The King continued to pursue his policy of allowing Catholics to occupy the highest offices in his Kingdoms and in 1687 he issued his "Declaration of Indulgence" in which he used his dispensing powers to cancel the effects of laws which punished Catholics and Protestant Dissenters. By now, almost everything he did or said served only to fuel controversy or feed the fires of discontent and revolution, or, in most cases, both; and he succeeded only in alienating the vast majority of his subjects. All this was irreversibly building towards the only possible outcomes, revolution, invasion and the termination of his own personal reign; the shortest of any of the Stewart monarchs at 57 days short of four years, and all of which came about with the Glorious Revolution on the 23rd of December 1688! Even today, historians are still at loggerheads as to whether James was an egotistical, tyrannical bigot or was he just plain naive, to the point of stupidity? A third option sees him as a well-intentioned and enlightened despot well ahead of his time! Take your pick!

James however, wasn't done yet! Now exiled and living in France for four months with his wife and son as the guests of Louis XIV, the deposed monarch decided on one last throw of the dice and landed in Ireland in March 1689 with 6,000 French troops. He spent the next fifteen months working to build an army of some 25,000 men which was composed mainly of poorly trained Irish and Scottish Jacobites to augment his French regiments. In June 1690 he advanced on Londonderry and met with the superior 36,000 strong forces of King William III at the river Boyne near Drogheda on the 12th of July and was heavily defeated, thus establishing subsequent

Protestant supremacy throughout Britain and Ireland! James fled once more to France departing Ireland from Kinsale and was never again to return to any of his former Kingdoms. After the battle he was Christened *Seamus an Chaca* or "James the Shit" amongst his previous Irish supporters who saw his flight as an act of desertion!

He saw out the rest of his life in exile at the royal chateau of Saint-Germain en Laye where he died of a brain haemorrhage on the 16th of September 1701. There had been an attempt to assassinate William III in 1696 to facilitate James's return but the plot failed and only served to make his cause even less popular. James continued to lay claim to the thrones of his Kingdoms right up to his death in 1701 when his son, James Francis Edward Stewart, "the old pretender" inherited the claims, calling himself James VIII &III of Scotland and England respectively even after these Kingdoms were merged and became the Kingdom of Great Britain; he was to stage a second Jacobite rebellion in 1715 which also failed as had the first one in July 1689. His son and James VII & II's grandson, Charles Edward Stewart, Charles III, "the young pretender" and "Bonnie Prince Charlie", staged a third Jacobite rebellion in 1745 but this was also doomed to failure.

The Stewart dynasty ground to a rather ignominious finale with the deaths of Charles III in 1788 and his brother Henry I in 1807, both men dying without legitimate issue and thus bringing the curtain down on some 436 years of captivating and fascinating history! We will have a closer look at these men and these later events in a final chapter after first investigating the penultimate joint monarchs of the dynasty, William and Mary, and their successor, the ultimate Stewart occupier of the throne, Queen Anne!

William of Orange, King William II & III, 1689 – 1702

Mary Stewart, Queen Mary II, 1689 – 1694

Before we continue with the central theme of this book, I am going to beg the reader's indulgence for five minutes here as I go off at something of a tangent and relate what I thought was a fascinating, if a tad frivolous, piece of information I came across in my research. In the late 17th and early 18th centuries, England, particularly London, was in the grip of a binge drinking epidemic known as the "Gin Craze" which took the best part of half a century and an act of parliament, the "Gin Act of 1736", to bring under control! What does this have to do with the price of eggs, I hear you ask? Well apparently, gin is an imitation of a Dutch spirit called "genever" which came over to England with William of Orange who promptly decided, for reasons unknown, to liberalise this country's home distilling laws! This gave rise to the population substituting the expensive ingredients of genever with the likes of turpentine and even sulphuric acid to produce cheap, English, rot-gut gin and unlicensed gin-shops flourished; at the height of the problem there was 17,000 gin shops in London alone, a city of over half a million even then, or one shop for every 35 people! Consumption by Londoners alone was estimated at eleven million gallons a year or two pints per person per week. Looking at these facts and figures from 300 years ago, the alcohol problems prevalent today, though serious, tend to pale almost into insignificance. Anyway, back to the story.

William III was Prince of Orange from his birth on the 4th of November 1650, as his father had died of smallpox a few days before he was born, and remained such until his death on the 8th of March 1702. He was also Stadtholder of Holland, Zeeland, Utrecht, Gelderland and Overijssel from July 1672 until his death and he formally accepted the English parliament's invitation to the thrones vacated by James VII & II on the 13th of February 1689, being crowned on the 11th of April that year. William was half Stewart despite being born in The Hague in Holland and his father being William II, Prince of Orange and Nassau. This was due to his mother being Mary,

Princess Royal, and eldest daughter of King Charles I of Scotland, England and Ireland. Mary and William III were wed on the 2nd of May 1641 in the Chapel Royal, Whitehall Palace, London; the marriage though, wasn't consummated for a few years as the bride was only nine years old at the time of her wedding! The fact that William's regnal number, III, is the same for England and Orange is pure coincidence; his regnal number for Scotland though is II.

Queen Mary II was born on the 30th of April 1662, daughter of King James VII & II and his first wife, Anne. She and her husband were also first cousins as well as joint monarchs of her deposed father's Kingdoms, from the 13th of February 1689 until her death of smallpox on the 28th of December 1694 and after which, William ruled alone, albeit a much sadder man. In Scotland, the Jacobites saw her death as divine retribution as they considered her to have broken the fifth commandment – *honour thy father* – both monarchs died without issue which meant that Mary's younger sister Anne was next in the Protestant line of succession as laid down by the "Bill of Rights of 1689"! Before that though, came "The Toleration Act of 1689" passed on the 24th of May by the English parliament and aimed at establishing freedom of worship for all non-conformists (to the C of E) except Catholics, thus rewarding Protestant dissenters for refusing to side with James VII & II!

The Bill of Rights 1689 (England) Act & the Claim of Rights 1689 (Scotland) Act!

After the Glorious Revolution, the Convention Parliament in England declared that James II had abdicated by fleeing the country on the 23rd of December 1688 and issued a forerunner of the Bill of Rights (passed as an act of parliament on the 16th of December 1689), the "Declaration if Rights" on the 13th of February 1689 offering the crown of England to William and Mary, all pretty straightforward, but not so in Scotland! As James VII had neither been present in Scotland during the crises and hadn't fled from there, it couldn't be held that he had abdicated his Scottish crown. Instead, a Convention of the Scottish Estates (a sister institution to the Scottish parliament) decided that he had forfeited it by his behaviour and so removed him from office on the 4th of April, offering it to William and Mary on the 11th of April and proclaiming them King William II and Queen Mary II of Scotland from that day, thus they simultaneously became the joint rulers of Scotland, England and Ireland!

The "Claim of Rights Act" issued by the Scottish Parliament in April 1689 was specifically aimed at "bolstering the position of parliament within the Scottish constitution at the expense of the royal prerogative", and served precisely the same purpose as its sister "Bill of Rights Act" in England, which was to severely curtail the powers of the reigning monarch(s) thus hopefully ensuring that the disasters, turmoil and wholesale carnage of the previous sixty four years, mostly instigated at the whims of megalomaniacs and religious bigots, could never again be repeated! Amongst other things, these acts set out the rules for the freedom of speech in both parliaments, the requirement for regular elections to both parliaments and the right to petition the monarch(s) without fear of retribution. They also re-established the liberty of Protestants to have arms for their defence within the rule of law and condemned James VII & II for his unfair and preferential treatment of Catholics whilst simultaneously persecuting Protestants, particularly Scottish Presbyterians!

These acts, in the entirety of their provisions, cannot be altered, even today, without the explicit consent of every realm and the acts, between them, went a long way towards the establishment of a constitutional monarchy within the United Kingdom today. They were also the predecessors of the French "Declaration of the Rights of Man and the Citizen", the United States "Bill of Rights", the Canadian "Charter of Rights and Freedoms", the UN "Declaration of Human Rights" and the "European Convention on Human Rights"! All this in spite of the fact that they seemed, at first glance anyway, to merely reverse James's jaundiced outlook by giving Protestants preferential treatment whilst persecuting Catholics!

These Bills even went so far as to state "it hath been found by experience that it is inconsistent with the safety and welfare of these Protestant Kingdoms to be governed by a Papist Prince"! Thus William II & III and Mary II were named as the successors of James VII & II and that the thrones would pass from them first to Mary's heirs, then to her sister Princess Anne of Denmark and her heirs, and then to any heirs of William by a later marriage. The monarch(s) were expressly forbidden to adopt Catholicism or even to marry a Catholic and were further required to swear a coronation oath to maintain the Protestant religion! These edicts were soon to be further stressed by future legislation.

The First Jacobite Rebellion

1689 to 1692, as well as being host to the momentous events of the Glorious Revolution and James's abdication in England, the Battle of the Boyne in Ireland and the succession of William and Mary to the thrones of the three Kingdoms, also saw the birth of the Jacobite cause in Scotland! These Jacobites (from the Latin "Jacobus" for James) were supporters of the now Catholic House of Stewart in general and the deposed James VII & II in particular against the Protestant Williamites or "Whigs". After their proclamation in Edinburgh on the 11th of April 1689, the joint monarchs had definitively accepted the Church of Scotland as a Presbyterian institution after decades of concerted attempts by James VI, Charles I, Charles II and James VII to mould it into an Episcopalian institution, thereby making it more acceptable (and pliable) to the royal control of those monarchs who chose to be Catholic!

This acceptance of William and Mary created a groundswell of opinion against the crown in Scotland which resulted in John Graham of Claverhouse, or "Bonnie Dundee" as he became known, raising the standard of James VII on Dundee Law on the 16th of April thus instigating the first Jacobite Rebellion. Graham was also known as "Bluidy Clavers" for his part in the defeat of the Protestant Covenanters at the Battles of Drumclog and Bothwell Brig in June 1679 while fighting for the Royalists. By July, Graham had eight battalions at his disposal as well as some 300 Irishmen sent over by James VII who was already in Ireland, to assist with the uprising. This got off to an excellent start at the Battle of Killicrankie on the 27th of July 1689 where the Jacobites routed a much superior Williamite force but at the cost of "Dundee" himself who fell mortally wounded in the battle!

These fortunes however were reversed at the Battle of Dunkeld some three weeks later where the Jacobites were routed by a conglomeration of Williamite troops, Covenanters and the Cameronians, an infantry regiment raised in 1688. Many skirmishes followed this until the Jacobites were again decisively beaten at "The Haugh's O' Cromdale" on the 1st of May 1690. When news came from Ireland a couple of months later of William's victory over James at the Battle of the Boyne, Jacobite hopes of any success began to fail! On the 17th of August 1691 King William II offered all the Highland clans a pardon for their part in the uprising; this though was on the proviso that they took an oath of allegiance before the 1st of January 1692 and in front of a magistrate! The Clan Chiefs sent word to James, now back in exile in France, asking for his permission to take this oath but it was mid-December before his reply, authorising them to do so, was received.

Some of the Chieftains managed to comply within the allotted time, but some, mainly due to the very inclement winter weather, did not. Among those was Alasdair MacLain, 12th Chief of the MacDonald's of Glencoe and he was the one that the Secretary of State over Scotland and Lord Advocate, John Dalrymple, Master of Stair, chose to make an example off. Lord Stair was a Lowlander who disliked Highlanders so he authorised the 1st and 2nd Companies of the Earl of Argyll's Regiment of Foot, under the command of Robert Campbell of Glenlyon to be mobilised and billeted upon the MacDonald's of Glencoe during the night of the 12th and 13th of February. The soldiers were welcomed into the villager's homes and given food and warmth; and the rest, as they say, is history! 38 MacDonald's were murdered, some in their beds, and approximately another 40, women and children amongst them, died of exposure whilst trying to escape the carnage!

The whole episode was later proved to have been premeditated at the highest level and charges of "murder under trust", a special
293

category of murder under Scots Law which covers the most heinous of crimes, was called upon to be brought against many of the perpetrators. Needless to say, the whitewash brush came out, ranks were closed and no-one was ever brought to task for the slaughter though many officials, high and low, were tainted for a long time afterwards, in some cases, for generations. The Glencoe Massacre became a Jacobite rallying call for the next generation of Stewart Royalists in the risings of 1715 and 1745 but it was to draw a line under this, the first of them!

The Demise of Queen Mary II

From 1690 onwards, William was often absent from England on campaign, generally each year from the spring until the autumn. In 1690, he fought the Jacobites in Ireland, and whilst her husband was away, Mary administered the government of the realm with the advice of a nine-member Cabinet Council. She was not keen to assume power and she felt "deprived of all that was dear to me in the person of my husband, left alone among those that were perfect strangers to me: my sister of a humour so reserved that I could have little comfort from her". Anne had quarrelled with William and Mary over money, and the relationship between
294

the two sisters had soured! William had crushed the Irish Jacobites by 1692, but he continued with campaigns abroad in order to wage war against France in the Netherlands. When her husband was away, Mary acted on her own if his advice was not available; whilst he was in England, Mary completely refrained from interfering in political matters, as had been agreed in the Declaration and Bill of Rights and as she preferred.

Mary proved a firm ruler, ordering the arrest of her own uncle, Henry Hyde, 2nd Earl of Clarendon, for plotting to restore James II to the throne. In January 1692, the influential John Churchill, 1st Earl of Marlborough, was dismissed on similar charges; the dismissal somewhat diminished her popularity and further harmed her relationship with her sister Anne (who was strongly influenced by Churchill's wife, Sarah). Anne appeared at court with Sarah, obviously supporting the disgraced Churchill, which led to Mary angrily demanding that Anne dismiss Sarah and vacate her lodgings. Mary fell ill with a fever in April, and missed Sunday church service for the first time in 12 years. She also failed to visit Anne, who was suffering a difficult labour. After Mary's recovery and the death of Anne's baby soon after it was born, Mary did visit her sister, but chose the opportunity to berate Anne for her friendship with Sarah. The sisters never saw each other again! Mary recorded in her journal that the breach between the sisters was a punishment from God for the "irregularity" of the Revolution. She was extremely devout, and attended prayers at least twice a day. Many of her proclamations focus on combating licentiousness, insobriety and vice. She often participated in the affairs of the Church—all matters of ecclesiastical patronage passed through her hands.

On the death of the Archbishop of Canterbury, John Tillotson on the 22nd of November 1694, Mary was keen to appoint the Bishop of Worcester, Edward Stillingfleet to the vacancy, but her husband overruled her and the post went to the Bishop of Lincoln, Thomas Tenison instead. Also in the early December of that year cane the "Triennial Act" which was a reinforcement of that part of the Bill of Rights which dealt with the summoning of parliament on a regular basis as well as ensuring frequent general elections, under this act, these had to occur at least once every three years. This however, led to some instability over a period of time and the "Septennial Act" replaced it in 1716 meaning a parliament could remain in being for up to seven years.

The Queen was tall for a woman at 5 foot 11 inches and apparently fit, she would regularly walk between her palaces at Whitehall and Kensington. In late 1694, however, she contracted smallpox. She sent away anyone who had not previously had the disease, to prevent the spread of infection and Anne, who was once again pregnant, sent Mary a letter saying she would run any risk to see her sister again, but the offer was declined by Mary's groom of the stole, the Countess of Derby. Mary died at Kensington Palace shortly after midnight on the morning of 28 December. While the Scottish Jacobites considered her death divine retribution for breaking the fifth commandment ("honour thy father"), she was generally widely mourned in Britain. During a cold winter, in which the Thames froze, her embalmed body lay in state in the Banqueting House at Whitehall. On 5 March 1695, she was buried at Westminster Abbey. Her funeral service was the first of any royal attended by all the members of both Houses of Parliament! For the ceremony, composer Henry Purcell wrote "Music for the Funeral of Queen Mary".

William, who had grown increasingly to rely on Mary, was devastated by her death, and was quoted as saying that "from being the happiest of men"; he was "now going to be the most miserable creature on earth". This however, didn't stop the scandal mongers from putting about unsubstantiated rumours regarding the King's sexual orientation over the next few years! Now the sole monarch of the three Kingdoms, William saw the advisability of selecting a ministry from the party with the majority in the Commons and appointed such in 1696 drawn from the Whigs. Known as "The Junto", it created suspicion from other MP's as it met separately but it could be regarded as the forerunner of today's "Cabinet of Ministers". Despite his conversion to Anglicanism, his popularity waned drastically, particularly north of the border, after Mary's death. This could also have had something to do with the fact that the latter half of the 1690's was blighted by famine in many parts of Scotland due to extremely wet weather as well as the economic climate! The complete collapse of the "Darien Project" which left the country bankrupt and impoverished the population also impacted very badly on the King.

This was one of those impossible, "pie in the sky", "get rich quick for virtually no outlay" schemes which are invariably doomed to disaster from the start. A Scottish trading colony under the leadership of Thomas Drummond and Alexander Campbell was established on the Isthmus of Panama in the Americas on the 2nd of November 1698 and called itself, grandiosely, "Caledonia", with a capitol town of "New Edinburgh"! To cut a long story short, the colony never achieved the status of a going concern and was finally abandoned in March 1700 as a total disaster to say nothing of the loss of some 2,000 lives. The Scots petitioned the King to make some attempt to rectify the deplorable financial situation but William declined, thereby seeing his popularity, or lack of it, plummet even further!

The Act of Settlement 1701 (England)

This was an act passed by the English parliament the main purpose of which was to reinforce the Bill of Rights 1689 regarding the Protestant succession to the throne and to strengthen the guarantees of a parliamentary system of Government. This act was passed on the 12th of July 1701 and by which time Queen Mary II had died childless seven years previously. Her sister Anne's last surviving child out of seventeen pregnancies, William Duke of Gloucester, had died aged eleven on the 30th of July 1700, and King William had not remarried and was not keeping good health! All this put the line of succession in serious jeopardy and decisions had to be made as Anne was now the last remaining claimant but there was no-one after her, no-one eligible anyway!

Taking everything into account, it was decided that the Princess Sophie, Electress of Hanover and granddaughter of James VI & I, and her Protestant heirs were the only plausible contenders after Anne as the act also lay down that no Roman Catholic could inherit the crown and no reigning monarch could marry a Catholic either. The sovereign also had to swear to uphold the Church of England (and after 1707 the Church of Scotland also). The act not only addressed the dynastic and religious aspects of succession, it also further restricted the powers and prerogatives of the crown such as establishing judicial independence in the courts and It also put paid, deliberately, to any hopes of the Catholic heirs of James VII & II ever re-inheriting! The Scottish parliament wasn't entirely happy with this act and its ramifications and was to reply with its own "Act of Security" in 1704.

King William, apparently never a man of robust health, died of pneumonia on the 8th of March 1702 as a result of breaking a collarbone in a fall from his horse. The animal had reputedly stumbled on a mole's burrow and because of this; the Jacobites raised their glasses and toasted "the little gentleman in the black velvet waistcoat" for a long time afterwards as an ironic and mocking gesture to their hated nemesis "King Billy", as he was affectionately – or otherwise – known, depending on one's own beliefs and religious standpoint, throughout his Kingdoms of Scotland and Ireland. Even today, in those two countries, William II & III is viewed as a hero and saviour by one camp and as a vicious, bloodthirsty despot by the other! Eleven months prior to William's death, James VII & II had died in exile in France leaving a son whom the French King, Louis XIV officially recognised as King James VIII & III of Scotland, England and Ireland.

Anne Stewart, Queen Anne, 1702 – 1714

This, the last of our Stewart monarchs, was born on the 6th of February 1665, the second daughter of James VII & II and his first wife, Anne Hyde. She became Queen of Scotland, England and Ireland on the 8th of March 1702 with the demise of King William II & III. Under the terms of the Acts of Union she became Queen of Great Britain and Ireland on the 1st of May 1707 when Scotland and England united as a single sovereign state and she remained such until her death, without issue, on the 1st of August 1714, thus bringing down the final curtain on the dynasty of the Royal House of Stewart! Under the terms of the Act of Settlement 1701, Anne was succeeded by her second cousin George I of the House of Hanover, who was a descendant of the Stewarts through his maternal grandmother, Elizabeth, daughter of King James VI & I. This was in spite of many stronger claims to the thrones, all Catholic, and not the least of which was Queen Anne's half brother, James Francis

Edward Stewart, son of James VII & II by his second (Catholic) wife!

In keeping with the traditions of the royal family at that time, Anne and her elder sister Mary were raised separated from their father in their own establishment in Richmond, London and on the strict instructions of their uncle, King Charles II, they were both raised as Protestants. Charles had more than a few problems finding a husband for his niece as on the one hand he had the appeasement of his Protestant subjects to consider and on the other he had to try and find one acceptable to his Catholic ally, King Louis XIV of France! The Danes were Protestant allies of France and an Anglo-Danish alliance to contain the power of the Dutch seemed like a good idea, so a marriage between Anne and Prince George of Denmark, the younger brother of King Christian V, was negotiated.

Anne's father, the Duke of York and future King James VII & II, was delighted with this arrangement as it diminished the influence of his other son-in-law, William of Orange, who had married Anne's sister Mary on the 4th of November 1677 and who was naturally displeased at the proposed match. The wedding went ahead anyway on the 28th of July 1683 in the Chapel Royal at Hampton Court Palace.

Although it was an arranged marriage, the two of them were apparently faithful and devoted partners and Anne was quickly pregnant. She was however to be plagued by ill-health throughout her life and despite a prolific seventeen pregnancies, she died without any surviving children. The last of these, William, Duke of Gloucester, always a weak and sickly child, had died of smallpox or possibly scarlet fever, aged eleven on the 30th of July 1700, just six months after Anne's final pregnancy ended in a miscarriage on the 25th of January that year. Anne was to grow increasingly lame and obese during her later years, particularly after the death of her husband in October 1708.

She was crowned Queen of Scotland, England and Ireland on St George's day, the 23rd of April 1702 and was carried to Westminster Abbey in an open sedan chair with a low back to allow her train to flow out behind her as even if these days, she suffered from gout! She appointed her husband Lord High Admiral, giving him control of the Royal navy and she appointed Lord Marlborough Captain-General of the Army, giving him control of that. His wife, the Duchess of Marlborough was appointed Groom of the Stole, Mistress of the Robes and Keeper of the Privy Purse. 1702 also saw Britain become embroiled in the "War of Spanish Succession" which had started the year before and continued to rage intermittently all over Europe until just after Anne's death in 1714. Happening simultaneously with this was "Queen Anne's War", being fought between Britain, France, Spain and several tribes of North American Indians on the eastern seaboards of Canada and America and which continued from 1702 until 1713. This period of history could actually lay claim to be the host of the "First World War" as several different countries were at conflict with each other on two different continents and the navies of these countries fought each other on many different seas and oceans!

In a nautical vein, 1703 (December the 12th to be exact) was the year of "The Great Storm"! This was a hurricane of unprecedented ferocity and duration which blew in from the south-west causing great damage and chaos across the entire country particularly the south-west and midlands of England. The barometer registered >950mB, the overall death toll on land and at sea was estimated at between 8,000 and 15,000 (up to quarter of a million in today's money), ships were lost at sea and destroyed in harbours, thousands of chimney stacks were blown down and whole roofs were ripped off, farm stock was destroyed in their thousands some just disappearing, rivers burst their banks and great swathes of countryside was flooded, the first Eddystone lighthouse was destroyed and the list just goes on and on! The disaster was seen as an act of God because of the "crying sins" of the nation and the government dedicated the 19th of January 1704 as a day of fasting in repentance!

Act of Security (Scotland) 1704 and the Acts of Union 1706 &1707

While Ireland was subordinate to the English Crown and Wales formed part of the kingdom of England, Scotland remained an independent sovereign state with its own parliament and laws. The Act of Settlement 1701, passed by the English Parliament, applied in the kingdoms of England and Ireland but not Scotland, where a strong minority wished to preserve the Stewart dynasty and its right of inheritance to the throne. Anne had declared it "very necessary" to conclude a union of England and Scotland in her first speech to the English Parliament, and a joint Anglo-Scots commission met to discuss terms in October 1702. The negotiations broke up in early February 1703 having failed to reach an agreement. The parliament of Scotland responded to the Act of Settlement by passing the "Act of Security 1704", which gave the it the power, if the Queen had no further children, to choose the next Scottish monarch from among the Protestant descendants of the royal line of Scotland. The individual chosen by the Estates could not be the same person who came to the English throne, unless England granted full freedom of trade to Scottish merchants. At first, Anne withheld royal assent to the act, but granted it the following year when the parliament threatened to withhold supply, endangering Scottish support for England's wars!

In its turn, the English parliament responded with the "Alien Act 1705", which threatened to impose economic sanctions and declare Scottish subjects aliens in England, unless Scotland either repealed the Act of Security or moved to unite with England. The Scottish parliament chose the latter option! The English Parliament agreed to repeal the Alien Act, and new commissioners were appointed by Queen Anne in early 1706 to negotiate the terms of a union. The articles of union approved by the commissioners were presented to Queen Anne on 23 July 1706, and ratified by the Scottish and English Parliaments on 16 January and 6 March 1707 respectively. Under the Acts of Union, England and Scotland were united into a single Kingdom called Great Britain, with one parliament on the 1st of May

1707! Anne, a consistent and ardent supporter of a union despite opposition on both sides of the border, attended a thanksgiving service in St Paul's Cathedral. The Scot Sir John Clerk, 1st Baronet, who also attended, wrote, "Nobody on this occasion appeared more sincerely devout and thankful than the Queen herself"!

The Acts of Union were swiftly put to the test when Anne's Catholic half brother, James Francis Edward Stewart, attempted to land in Scotland with French assistance at the Firth of Forth on the 23rd of March 1708 in an attempt to establish himself as King. James had declared himself King James VIII & III of Scotland, England and Ireland on the death of his father in 1701 and was recognised as such by France, Spain and the Papal States who also refused to recognise William, Mary or Anne as legitimate sovereigns! A "Scottish Militia Bill" had been passed aimed at arming the local Scots against such a landing but Anne withheld royal assent for fear of any militia raised being disloyal and siding with the Jacobites. The small invasion fleet never landed so James never set foot on Scottish soil; the French Admiral had turned and ran rather than risk a naval battle with an English fleet which was closing on him. As a result of claiming his father's thrones, James had earlier been attainded for treason in London on the 2nd of March 1702 and his titles declared forfeit!

In the meantime, the War of Spanish Succession was rumbling on unabated across Europe and the Grand Alliance forces of Scotland, England (later Britain), the Holy Roman Empire, Prussia, Austria and Holland, under its commander-in-chief John Churchill, 1st Duke of Marlborough, strung together decisive victories over their protagonists France, the Electorate of Bavaria and Bourbon Spain. These were Blenheim in August 1704, Ramillies in May 1706, Oudenarde in July 1708 and Malplaquet in September 1709! Despite these victories however, Marlborough fell from grace with Queen Anne in 1710 due to a bitter and violent quarrel between the Queen and his wife Sarah Churchill who was subsequently dismissed from court. The Duke remained in the wilderness until the succession of the House of Hanover with George I in 1714.

"Queen Anne's War" on the eastern seaboards of the North American continent was also still rumbling on, up until a preliminary peace in 1712 set the stage for the "Treaty of Utrecht" in 1713 which finally ended the hostilities. Under this, the French conceded their claims to The Hudson Bay area, Acadia and Newfoundland to Britain whilst retaining Cape Breton and other Islands in the Gulf of St Lawrence. Some of the Treaties terms were a bit ambiguous however, and the concerns of the various Indian Tribes were not taken into account either which only set the stage for further, future conflicts.

Towards the end of her life Anne had lost all mobility due to severe gout and obesity, to the extent that after her demise she was buried in an almost square coffin! At her death, her family loyalty came to the fore and she was convinced that she should be succeeded by her Catholic half-brother, James Francis Edward Stewart, known as the "Old Pretender"! This of course was a non-starter due to the Bill of Rights 1689 and its reinforcement in the Act of Settlement 1701, the Queen had no say in the matter! This did however; give substance to the rumours that the Queen had harboured secret Jacobean tendencies earlier in her life despite the fact that the only time she was ever in Scotland was as a fifteen year old in 1680. The Electress Sophia of Hanover had died two months before Anne on the 8th of June 1714 which meant that her son, George I now inherited the thrones of Great Britain and Ireland.

In the opinion of many historians, traditional assessments of Anne as being fat, constantly pregnant, under the influence of favourites, and lacking political astuteness or interest probably derive from the rampant male chauvinist prejudices of the day against women! One such noted, "Hers was not, as used to be supposed, a petticoat government; she had considerable power; yet time and time again she had to capitulate". Another such concluded that Anne was often able to impose her will, even though as a woman in an age of male dominance, and preoccupied by her health, her reign was marked by an increase in the influence of parliamentary ministers and a decrease in the influence of the Crown. She attended more cabinet meetings than any of her predecessors or successors, and presided over an age of artistic, literary, economic and political advancement that was made possible only by the stability and prosperity of her reign!

King George I, George Louis of the House of Hanover, and great-grandson of King James VI & I of Scotland, England and Ireland, ascended to the thrones of Great Britain and Ireland on the 1st of August 1714 and reigned until his death on the 11th of June 1727! He was Queen Anne's closest living Protestant relative!

Jacobite Uprisings of 1715 and 1745

The last throws of the dice for the dynasty of the Royal House of Stewart! These were the second and third uprisings, being preceded, of course, by a first one, starting in 1688 and which was aimed at reinstating James VII & II but failed (see the chapter on William and Mary). This was followed by a rather vainglorious attempt in 1708 which never really got off the ground and so really fails to classify as an "uprising" (see the chapter on Queen Anne); this was aimed at re-establishing the house of Stewart as the next in line for succession to the thrones of Great Britain and Ireland with James VIII & III! It should be remembered here that the line of succession to the thrones had been settled in England, for the foreseeable future, with the Act of Settlement 1701 and that the Acts of Union 1707 applied that Act of Settlement 1701 to Scotland as well, under the jurisdiction of the Parliament of Great Britain circa the 1st of May 1707, whether the Jacobites liked it or not!

The first of the two we are looking at here was referred to as either "The Fifteen" or "Lord Mar's Revolt", and was quite simply aimed at replacing George I and the House of Hanover with James VIII & III - still in exile in France and now known as "The Pretender" - and the Royal House of Stewart!   On the 14th of March 1715, James appealed to Pope Clement XI for his help with a Jacobite uprising saying "It is not so much for a devoted son, oppressed by the injustices of his enemies, as a persecuted Church threatened with destruction, which appeals for the protection and help of its worthy Pontiff"!   It is considered doubtful but is also unclear if James ever received any backing, of any kind, from this quarter.

Sir John Erskine, Earl of Mar, despite receiving no commission from James to initiate hostilities but deprived of office by the new King George I, went in disguise from London to Scotland on the 27th of August and held the first council of war with many Highland chieftains at Aboyne in Aberdeenshire.   It was at Braemar, ten days later, on the 6th of September and in front of 600 supporters, that he raised the Standard of James VIII & III as a declaration of intent by proclaiming him King of Scotland, England, France and Ireland.   Erskine, self-appointed leader of the

Jacobites, was the 22nd Earl since its first creation in 1114, the 11th Earl since its second creation in 1426 and the 6th Earl since its seventh creation in 1565. He was somewhat contemptuously nicknamed "Bobbing John" for his well known tendency to flit back and forth between the Tories and the Whigs, and also between the Hanoverians and the Jacobites as the mood, or the flavour of the day, took him.

Mar's nemesis and opposite number during "the fifteen" was John Campbell, 2nd Duke of Argyll who, unlike Mar, was a proven and experienced military leader and General. He had served on the continent during the nine years war and had fought in the War of Spanish Succession. He was given command of all British troops in Spain during their successful evacuation and returned home to be made Commander in Chief, Scotland and subsequently led the Government forces against Mar at the Battle of Sheriffmuir. In short, Campbell was as efficient and experienced in the not so subtle art of warfare as Mar was a failure so the two were not only incompatible but also ill-matched!

The forces under Mar's command were gradually augmented, and initially were successful taking Inverness, Aberdeen, Dundee and Gordon Castle though they were unable to capture Fort

William. By the October, Mar's forces which now numbered 20,000, had all of Scotland above the Firth of Forth under their control and on the 22nd, James officially commissioned him commander of the Jacobite army. Whether this caused a rush of blood to the head or not really isn't quite clear, but Mar then decided to march on Stirling Castle, clashing with Campbell's government troops en route at Sheriffmuir on the 13th of November! The actual fighting here was indecisive but Campbell was deemed to have won the day as he was outnumbered three to one, Mar then retreated to Perth.

On the same day as Sheriffmuir, Inverness surrendered to Hanoverian forces and a smaller Jacobean force led by Mackintosh of Borlum was defeated at the Battle of Preston. Mackintosh's numbers had been boosted by the addition of Scottish Borderer Jacobites under William Gordon, 6th Viscount Kenmure, and a sizeable contingent of English Jacobites led by some minor English peers. This combination actually won the first day of the battle, inflicting heavy casualties on the Hanoverians but substantial government reinforcements arrived and the Jacobites eventually surrendered.

The Pretender, James VIII, landed in Scotland at Peterhead on the 22nd of December but by the time he reached Perth on the 9th of January 1716, the Jacobite army numbered less than 5,000. In contrast to this, Argyll's forces had grown, acquired heavy artillery and were advancing swiftly. On the 30th of January Mar led his men northwards out of Perth and on the 4th of February James wrote a farewell letter to Scotland, sailing for France from Montrose on the 5th. Many Jacobites were taken prisoner, tried for treason and sentenced to death but the "Indemnity Act" of 1717 eventually pardoned most of these! Others had their lands or estates confiscated and many of the rank and file was transported overseas. James VIII, "The Old Pretender", never returned and died in exile on the 1st of January 1766. The cause lost, Mar also fled to France with the Prince and he died in May 1732 in Paris.

"The Forty Five" and Culloden

This was a final attempt by a Stewart, the Old Pretender's son, Prince Charles Edward Stewart, known as "The Young Pretender" or as "Bonnie Prince Charlie", to overthrow the house of Hanover; replace King George II and put the Stewarts, in the shape of his father James VIII, back on the thrones of Great Britain and Ireland, he probably fancied himself as King Charles III at some future date as well! Born on the 31st of

319

December1720, he also, like his father and grandfather before him, died in exile but in Rome, not France, on the 31st of December 1788 and is buried in St Peter's Basilica in the Vatican City!

In December 1743, Charles's father named him Prince Regent, thereby authorising him to act in his name. Eighteen months later, the Prince led a French-backed rebellion intended to place his father on the thrones of Great Britain and Ireland. Charles raised funds to fit out two ships: the Elisabeth (not mis-spelt), an old man-of-war of 66 guns, and the Doutelle (le Du Teillay) a small frigate of 16 guns, which successfully landed him and seven companions at Eriskay on the 23rd of July 1745. Charles had hoped for support from a French fleet, but it was badly damaged by storms, and he was left stranded to raise an army in Scotland. The Jacobite cause was still supported by many Highland clans, mostly Catholic but also some Protestant. Charles hoped for a warm welcome from these clans to start an insurgency by Jacobites throughout Britain and duly raised his father's standard at Glenfinnan, gathering a force large enough to enable him to march on Edinburgh.

The city, under the control of the Lord Provost Archibald Stewart, quickly surrendered and while he was in the city, Charles's portrait was painted by the artist Allan Ramsay. On his way there, on the 21st of September, he defeated the only government army in Scotland at that time - most of the British Army was on the continent, involved in the War of Austrian Succession - at the Battle of Prestonpans. This army was led by General Sir John Cope, and their disastrous defence against the Jacobites is immortalised in the song "Hey Johnnie Cope are ye waukin yet" which refers to a silent, pre-dawn attack on the slumbering government troops resulting much slaughter for few casualties in return! By the 8th of November, after a lengthy wait during which he convinced his generals that the English Jacobites would rise and join them, Charles was marching south at the head of 6,000 men. He was also convinced that France would launch an invasion of England as well, but unfortunately, neither of these suppositions came to fruitition!

They advanced through Carlisle and Manchester to Derby and into a position where they appeared to threaten London itself, having met only with token resistance on the way. It was alleged at this stage that the King had made plans to decamp to Hanover but there is no actual evidence of this and indeed, the King is on record as stating that he would lead the troops against the rebels personally if they approached London! Reports were now being received in the Jacobite camp that the armies of Field Marshall George Wade and the King's son, the Duke of Cumberland were approaching, in all, London was defended by some 6,000 infantry, 700 horse and 33 artillery pieces, out with Wade's and Cumberland's troops! The Jacobite hierarchy were also much disturbed by reports of a third army marching on them; this was later proven to be a deliberate misinformation!

It was enough however for the Jacobite general, Lord George Murray and his council of war to insist upon returning to Scotland to join up with their growing forces there. On the 6th of December they withdrew, with a much aggrieved Prince, who actually had little or no experience of warfare on this scale, relinquishing command to Murray! In October, Wade had focussed his troops on Newcastle upon Tyne on the East coast of England to await the Scots; however the Jacobite forces had advanced from Scotland down the West coast of England via Carlisle into Lancashire and the speed of their advance left Wade scrambling. In freezing conditions and with his men starving, he failed to counter their march into England or their subsequent retreat, back the same way, from Derby to Scotland.

Wade was subsequently replaced as Commander-in-Chief with Prince William, Duke of Cumberland who led the army to success at the Battle of Culloden in April 1746.

On the long march back to Scotland, the Highland Army wore out its boots and demanded all the boots and shoes of the townspeople of Dumfries, as well as money and hospitality. The Jacobites reached Glasgow on the 25th of December where they were again reprovisioned, having threatened to sack the city, and were joined by a few thousand additional men; they then went on to defeat the forces of General Henry Hawley at the Battle of Falkirk Muir. The Duke of Cumberland arrived in Edinburgh on the 30th of January to take over command of the government army from General Hawley. He then marched north along the coast, with his army being kept supplied by sea. Six weeks were then spent at Aberdeen in training. The King's forces continued to pressurise Murray who retired north, losing men and failing to take either Stirling Castle or Fort William; but he did succeed in taking both Fort Augustus and Fort George in Inverness-shire in early April. Charles, against better advice, then decided to take command again, and insisted on setting up to fight a defensive action!

Hugh Rose, baron of Kilravock, entertained both Charles Edward Stuart and the Duke of Cumberland respectively on the 14th and 15th of April 1746 at his home, Kilravock Castle, on the eve of the Battle of Culloden on the 16th. Charles's manners and deportment were described by his host as most engaging; having walked out with the baron, he watched trees being planted and remarked, "How happy, sir, you must feel, to be thus peaceably employed in adorning your mansion, whilst all the country around it is in such commotion." Kilravock was a firm supporter of the house of Hanover, but his adherence was not solicited, nor was his preferences alluded to! The next day, the Duke of Cumberland called at the castle gate, and when Kilravock went to receive him, the Duke bluffly observed, "So you had my cousin Charles here yesterday." Kilravock replied, "What am I to do sir, I am Scots", to which Cumberland replied, "You did perfectly right sir"!

The Adversaries and the Battle

Nowhere is it better demonstrated than here, at Culloden, the statement I made earlier about religion (being man made and therefore flawed) rearing its ugly head and segregating families, friends and whole nations, more completely and finally than any other reason, be it personal or

324

political! Contrary to popular belief, this wasn't a Scotland V England confrontation; this was the culmination of two hundred years of festering, Catholic V Protestant bigotry and the really sad thing about it all is the fact that the uprising, for one reason or another was already dead on its feet before a shot was fired here, it was all a rather pointless exercise! Another popular and somewhat romantic misconception is that this was the biggest military disaster ever to befall Scotland; rubbish! That dubious honour lies with the Battle of Flodden fought in 1513 (see the chapter on James IV) where Scotland lost a whole generation of royalty and nobility, not to mention ten times the rank and file casualties sustained here at Culloden, which numbered approximately 2,000!

The Jacobite army was mainly comprised of 75% Highlanders bolstered with Lowland Scots, a detachment of English from the Manchester regiment, (another not well known fact), a battalion of Irish Piquet's, a French regiment of "Royal Ecossias" and was predominately Catholic or at least Episcopalian. They numbered about 7,000 including 60 odd cavalry, against Cumberland's 8,000 foot and 200 cavalry. Their principal commanders were Prince Charles Edward Stewart, Lord George Murray, James

Drummond Duke of Perth, Lord John Drummond of Perth and John Roy Stewart, a distinguished Officer and Jacobite. One of the main problems with Charles's army was the dearth of trained and experienced officers, who often had difficulty controlling their men, particularly the fiery Highlanders. Another problem was the availability of weaponry; again the romantic image of the broadsword swinging Highlander is no more than just that, an image. After the battle only 200 were recovered which equated to less than 20% being armed with them, most carried the ancient and cumbersome firelock musket or pikes or other makeshift arms such as pitchforks!

The Government army was made up of 16 infantry battalions, 5 of whom were composed of mainly Lowland but also some Highland Scots, another 2 of German Hessians and Austrians and a battalion of Ulstermen, the rest, English. These were predominately Protestant and Presbyterian and were led by the King's son, William Augustus, Duke of Cumberland who was later to become known as "the butcher Cumberland" and whose title was to die with him in disgrace in 1765. That particular Dukedom was never to be recreated! His principal commanders were Major General Humphrey Bland, Major General

William Anne 2nd Earl of Albemarle (no relation to General George Monck, created Duke of Albemarle in 1660), General John Huske, Brigadier John Mordaunt and finally, General Evelyn Pierrepoint, the 2nd Duke of Kingston.

This latter was in command of the "Duke of Kingston's Regiment of Horse" and was responsible, directly or indirectly, for much of the indiscriminate slaughter of refugees from the battle upon its completion, as well as innocent women and children up to 3 miles from the battlefield! His regiment, only just raised prior to the battle, was ignominiously disbanded after it for their atrocious behaviour! Interestingly, Cumberland, who was himself directly or indirectly responsible for slaughtering the Jacobite wounded as they lay on the battlefield, saw fit to recruit Kingston's disgraced men into his own newly formed, "Duke of Cumberland's Regiment of Light Dragoon's" in September 1746! Both of these men have since, deservedly, been recognised in the annals of history for what they were!

Before the onset of the battle proper, Charles and Murray were at loggerheads. Charles had assumed command and had unilaterally chosen the field of battle which Murray and other senior officers did not like, and they tried in vain to point out the rough moorland terrain favoured Cumberland's artillery but could only hamper the famous "Highland Charge". Charles, like many of his forbears, refused to be counselled! At Murray's suggestion, it was decided to try for a repeat of "Prestonpans" with a night assault on the Hanoverian lines but this, due to poor leadership and worse decisions, failed dismally and led only to a tired, hungry and confused army lining up against a fresh, rested and well fed one the following morning! Without going into detail, of which there is plenty, it is suffice to say that a leaderless Jacobite army – Charles and Murray could no longer stand the sight of each other by this time – was routed and put to the sword in just over four hours. Any decisions made that day, as on the previous night, were invariably made by Charles and, just as invariably, were proven to be erroneous at best, disastrous at worse!

Charles then deserted both his cause and his men, fleeing the field and swearing to "return with an army" at some ambiguous future date. He slowly made his way west taking almost a year to reach Arisaig on the west coast of Scotland as he spent a lot of his time in hiding. For many months he criss-crossed the land, constantly under threat from either Government supporters or local Lairds who were tempted to betray him for the £30,000 bounty on his head! During this time he famously met Flora MacDonald who ferried him to Skye and finally, on the 19th of September 1747, he reached Borrodale on Loch Nan Uamh in the Sound of Arisaig where he boarded a French ship and sailed for the continent, never to return! Thus the final line was drawn, somewhat ignominiously, under the dynasty of the Royal House of Stewart!

The Acts of Union 1800

It only remains now, as I said many thousands of words ago, to cross the T's and dot the I's with a brief run-down of the "Acts of Union 1800" and what it means to these British Isles. Basically, these were two complimentary acts namely:

The "Union with Ireland Act 1800", an act of the Parliament of Great Britain, and:

The "Act of Union (Ireland) 1800", an act of the Parliament of Ireland.

These were passed on the 2nd of July 1800 and the 1st of August 1800 respectively and the twin acts united the Kingdom of Great Britain and the Kingdom of Ireland to create the "United Kingdom of Great Britain and Ireland" which came into effect on the 1st of January 1801 and remain in force, though since amended, in the UK today!

In the Republic of Ireland, the first act, passed in Great Britain, was formally repealed by the Oireachtas in 1983 with the passing of the

"Statute Law Revision Act". The second act, passed in Ireland, was repealed in 1962. The Oireachtas is the National Parliament of the Republic of Ireland and consists of 2 houses, the Senate and the House of Representatives!

Before these Acts, Ireland had been in personal union with England since 1541, when the Irish Parliament had passed the Crown of Ireland Act 1542, proclaiming King Henry VIII of England to be King of Ireland. Before then, since the 12th century, the King of England had been overlord of the Lordship of Ireland which was a papal possession. Both Ireland and England had come in personal union with Scotland with the Union of the Crowns in 1603. In 1707, the Kingdom of England and the Kingdom of Scotland were united into a single Kingdom: the Kingdom of Great Britain. Upon that union, each House of the Parliament of Ireland passed a congratulatory address to Queen Anne, praying that, "May God put it in your royal heart to add greater strength and lustre to your crown, by a still more comprehensive Union". The Irish parliament at that time was subject to a number of restrictions that placed it subservient to the Parliament of England and, following the union of England and Scotland, the Parliament of Great Britain.

In the century that followed the union of England and Scotland, Ireland gained effective legislative independence from Great Britain through the Constitution of 1782. However, access to institutional power in Ireland was restricted to a small minority, the so-called Protestant Ascendancy, and frustration at the lack of reform eventually led to a rebellion in 1798, involving a French invasion of Ireland and the seeking of complete independence from Great Britain. The rebellion was crushed with much bloodshed, and the subsequent drive for union between Great Britain and Ireland that passed in 1800, was motivated at least in part, by the belief that the rebellion had been caused as much by loyalist brutality as by the United Irishmen.

Each of these Acts had to be passed in the Parliament of Great Britain as well as the Parliament of Ireland and after centuries of subordination to the English, and later, British Parliaments, the Parliament of Ireland gained a large measure of independence in the Constitution of 1782. Many members of the Irish Parliament jealously guarded its autonomy (notably Henry Grattan) and a motion for union was rejected in 1799. However, a concerted campaign by the British government eventually overcame the reluctance of the Irish Parliament.

Only Anglicans were permitted to become members of the Parliament of Ireland, though the great majority of the Irish population were Roman Catholic, with many Presbyterians in Ulster. In 1793 Roman Catholics regained the right to vote if they owned or rented property worth £2 p.a. The Catholic hierarchy was strongly in favour of union, hoping for rapid emancipation – the right to sit as MPs – which was however, delayed until 1829.

From the perspective of Great Britain, the union was required because of the uncertainty that followed the Irish Rebellion of 1798 which was inspired by the French Revolution of 1789 (that of the Bastille and the Guillotine), and gave the rebels justification. If Ireland adopted Catholic Emancipation, willingly or not, a Roman Catholic parliament could break away from Britain and ally with the French, while the same measure within a united kingdom would exclude that possibility. Also the Irish and British Parliaments, when creating the regency during King George III's "madness", gave the Prince Regent (the Prince of Wales and future George IV) different powers. These considerations led Great Britain to decide to merge the two kingdoms and their Parliaments.

The final passage of the Act in the Irish Parliament was achieved with substantial majorities, achieved in part, according to contemporary documents through bribery, namely the awarding of peerages and honours to critics to get their votes. Whereas the first attempt had been defeated in the Irish House of Commons by 109 votes against to 104 for, the second vote in 1800 produced a much more favourable result of 158 to 115! Part of the attraction of the Union for many Irish Catholics was the promise of Catholic Emancipation, thereby allowing for Roman Catholic MPs, which had not been allowed in the Irish Parliament. This was however blocked by King George III who argued that emancipating Roman Catholics would breach his Coronation Oath, and was therefore not realised until 9 years after his death in 1829!

Footnote

I hope the reader found this book to be a comprehensive compilation of historical facts – with not a little supposition and imagination thrown in - gleaned from many different sources, history books and the internet amongst them, collated, and then presented, hopefully, in a mentally stimulating format which the average reader, with any interest in the history of the British Isles at all, will have found it worthwhile to peruse. I have tried to keep the book as factual as possible, without getting too bogged down in a quagmire of facts and figures, and apologise unreservedly for any errors or accidental misrepresentations whish have unwittingly crept in. I have also endeavoured to retain my objectivity and to stay non-judgemental and unopinionated throughout. Where I have encountered conflicting information I have employed a "majority verdict" method of deciding the facts of the matter, in other words, where say two, out of three sources have agreed on what actually happened; that's what I have gone along with!

337

On that subject, I stated in the Foreword of this book that the change of spelling of the name "Stewart" to "Stuart" came about in the reign of Mary, Queen of Scots, and simply because the letter "W" does not exist in the French alphabet! I stumbled across a statement later on in my research that this change actually took place earlier on, somewhere in Lord Darnley's genealogy. After an in-depth investigation I found that the name "Stewart" remains constant in both Mary's and Darnley's lines of descent right from their common ancestor, Alexander Stewart of Dundonald, 4th High Steward of Scotland 1214 – 1283, through to Darnley's father, Mathew Stewart, 4th Earl of Lennox! This covers, in his case, a transition of some fourteen generations through many name and title changes but ultimately ends up back at the beginning with "Stewart". This leads me to surmise that Mary, being the senior partner so to speak, and being more French than Scots, imposed her will here on Darnley and decreed that their name would be spelt the French way from hereonin. I personally have stuck with "Stewart" as I declared in the Foreword!

Having reached approximately the two thirds stage of this historical and literary offering on the 19th of September 2014, I feel it is fitting to insert here a paragraph or two about the recent momentous events in this country's (Scotland's) history and the results of them on the United Kingdom today! In the first place, it wasn't just all about Scotland, it was very much about the United Kingdom as a whole and the fact that the Acts of Union 1706 and 1707 were put in serious jeopardy by none other than David Cameron, that Eton educated gentleman, who decided to take on Alec Salmond, the well known street fighter and dirty tricks merchant, in single combat to thrash out the precise terms of the up-coming referendum, and came off very much second best! He conceded five massive points which could have caused the break-up of the 307 year old union and put the long term prospects of the British Isles into terminal decline! And this could possibly all have come about by one, single, solitary vote!

The first of these was giving the vote to sixteen to eighteen year-olds, show me someone of that age and I'll show you someone who thinks they know it all but in fact know little and totally lack any experience.   Secondly comes the disenfranchising of about a million Scottish born Scots living in other parts of the UK who should have been entitled to a postal vote about the future of their nation of birth. Thirdly, there was no minimum turnout or poll majority stipulated, ideally, it should have required sixty per cent of a seventy per cent turnout to be declared legal, as it was, a single vote could have swung it either way. Cameron's fourth major faux-pas was allowing a "Yes – No" answer, "Agree – Disagree" would have been much fairer as any psychologist will tell you that no-one likes to be seen to say "No". The final point was in the wording of the question; "Should Scotland be Independent"; this is begging for a "Yes" reply, a much more neutral "Should Scotland leave the United Kingdom", would have been far more acceptable to everyone concerned!

Despite all that, for me at least, the electorate of Scotland returned the right decision and these recent events, I believe, were very much pertinent to the subject matter and general tone of this book as a whole, as they merely underline, again, how the rampant, tunnel visioned egotism of a few individuals can seriously damage the health of a nation and its people! If any clarity, or comparison, is required on these moot points, I am happy to recommend the reader to the relevant chapters on Charles I and James VII as well Cromwell's behaviour during the Interregnum, particularly in Ireland!

To finish, what comes across very strongly to me is the fact that we (the human race) never learn. All the mistakes made during the Stewarts reign are still being made today, just by different people, as the Bard commented, "Man has an infinite capacity for his inhumanity to Man"! I leave you with that sobering thought!

32425738R00195